Experience as an Art Form

Experience as an Art Form

Hypnosis, Hyperempiria, and the Best Me Technique

Don E. Gibbons, Ph.D.

Authors Choice Press

San Jose New York Lincoln Shanghai

Experience as an Art Form
Hypnosis, Hyperempiria, and the Best Me Technique

Authors Choice Press
an imprint of iUniverse.com, Inc.

For information address:
iUniverse.com, Inc.
5220 S 16th, Ste. 200
Lincoln, NE 68512
www.iuniverse.com

ISBN: 0-595-17308-X

Printed in the United States of America

TO ANNETTE AND KATHLEEN

Contents

Introduction

Just as a painter works with brush on canvas, and a sculptor works with chisel upon stone, this book shows the therapist how to utilize a dramatic new procedure to work with the most responsive medium of all, **experience as the mind perceives it.**

The book shows the therapist how to utilize a dramatic new procedure, the Best Me technique, which has many possible applications in the area of behavioral regulation and self-control by enabling a client to more fully experience in the present many of the satisfactions which are normally associated only with goal attainment.

The Best Me technique may also be utilized in sex therapy to maximize fulfillment between couples. Most people approach the end of life with a few treasured memories of special, loving moments which live on in the mind forever. Now imagine what memories your clients will carry into their later years **after** you have taught them how to create such special moments together whenever they wish. That is exactly what this book is going to show you how to do.

The book also presents a proposal for an alternative paradigm to the current clinical/counseling paradigm, in which the dramatic effects produced by suggestion lend themselves to the consideration of human experience itself as the ultimate medium for the creative artist. Applications of the Best Me technique within the new paradigm are discussed, recognizing that the ultimate purpose of art is identical with the ultimate purpose of therapy, namely, the facilitation of personal growth, the ennoblement of the human spirit, and the enrichment of human existence.

1 The Power of Suggestion

If you have ever watched the volunteers in a stage hypnosis show eagerly devouring a raw onion after being told that it is an apple, or deeply inhaling the fumes of pure ammonia after it has been described to them as fine perfume, or laughing uproariously after the hypnotist has said that the volunteers will see him dressed in a Santa Claus suit and hat, you have seen a first-hand demonstration of the power of suggestion. In fact, the effects produced are often so dramatic that some people in the audience may think, "This isn't real. Those people must be paid by the hypnotist to carry on like that." But social scientists who conduct research in the area of suggestion would be quick to disagree, pointing out that statistically, there are many potential volunteers in any large audience who **are** able to respond to such outlandish suggestions; and that the use of paid assistants is unnecessary.

Other people watching these goings-on may be inclined to dismiss them with a shrug, thinking, "That's all just the workings of the imagination." But if, by referring to the results as "imaginary," they are somehow implying that they are not "real," then these observers are dead wrong; for what is popularly referred to as the imagination is actually a group of very powerful mental abilities, which some people have in surprising abundance. In fact, the real effects produced by the workings of suggestion upon the imagination are powerful enough to allow its use, in the form of hypnosis, as a substitute for a general anesthetic to amputate limbs, extract teeth, and deliver babies by Caesarian section, usually with no pain whatever experienced by sufficiently responsive patients.

Just exactly what is suggestion, and how does it work? Let me illustrate the answer to these questions by means of an example. Suppose you are standing in front of a newspaper rack, about to buy a paper, when your eye is suddenly caught by the following headlines:

MASSIVE COMET POISED TO STRIKE EARTH
TOTAL DESTRUCTION FORECAST
MILLIONS GATHERING TO PRAY

A bolt of fear and alarm shoots through you as you stand rooted to the spot, paralyzed with apprehension—until you hear the sound of loud laughter behind you and, turning, you see a friend who seems to be thoroughly amused by your reaction, and you realize that you have been made the object of a practical joke. Your friend obviously placed this bogus newspaper in the rack on top of the others when he saw you coming.

A practical joke such as this one would be based on the principle of suggestion—that is, presenting an idea in such a way that it will be accepted as literally true, and therefore real But notice two things in particular about this illustration: if you really had been made the object of such a practical joke, you would have responded **totally**, not just with the responses you can make voluntarily, such as thinking about a place to hide, but with your involuntary responses as well: muscle tremor, dryness in the mouth, feeling frightened, and so on. And you would have responded **completely**, with the strength and intensity of your response appropriate to the strength of the idea which was suggested. In the imaginary situation just described, your friend made use of the power of suggestion to alter your basic perceptions of reality, which caused you to respond totally and completely in order to bring about the results he wanted. In other words, the power of suggestion is rooted in our perception of reality itself.

Suggestion and "Positive Thinking"

The first popular use of suggestion as a means of actualizing human potential was initiated by the French pharmacist, Émile Coué, who taught that the "unconscious mind" was most receptive during the moments when a person was hovering between wakefulness and sleep. If one were able and willing to take full advantage of the opportunity thus afforded for direct communication with the "unconscious," it would be possible to divest oneself completely of all the negative thoughts and feelings which had accumulated over the course of a lifetime and which were preventing a person from realizing his or her true potential. The way to accomplish this mental housecleaning, Coué believed, was to use these crucial moments between sleeping and wakefulness to repeat silently over and over to oneself the affirmation, "Every day, and in every way, I am getting better and better!"

Coué's teaching was initially received with a considerable amount of enthusiasm; and numerous individuals readily attested to dramatic improvements in their lives, attributing such changes to the faithful use of this technique. But as more and more people came to try it and found that it did not seem to work for them, Couéism soon fell into decline.

Every few years since the advent of Coué's technique, a new "positive thinking" movement has made its appearance. Recently, such movements have frequently taken the form of a series of seminars or workshops, structured in such a manner that the main purpose of each workshop is to give the participants a few tantalizing bits of information to whet their appetite to sign up for the next one. These workshops generally tend to follow the same set formula. First, they make use of a new and appealing name which sets the current technique apart from those which have gone before. Then, like its forerunners, each new system asserts that all human beings possess a vast reservoir of untapped abilities. A ritual or a set of exercises is usually emphasized which, it is asserted, will enable the participants to actualize this potential if the procedures set forth are faithfully and diligently followed; and finally, some portion of the workshops is devoted to a collection of anecdotes and/or testimonials illustrating how the new technique has indeed changed people's lives for the better, bringing health and prosperity to those who were formerly devoid of hope.

Just as a properly timed and appropriately delivered pep talk can occasionally transform a losing athletic team into a winning one, so can a belief in positive thinking occasionally shift an individual from a losing to a winning pattern in the battle of life. Such persons can be expected to attempt eagerly to spread the word to others concerning the degree to which the new system has been of help to them. But as more and more people come to try the new technique and find that, as far as they are concerned, its effects are only temporary, the method rapidly begins to lose popularity and the stage is set for the next positive thinking movement to come along a few years later.

The principal reason why such approaches have only been effective with a minority of the general population is the inability of those using these systems to distinguish between situations for which the particular suggestions and philosophies they contain are appropriate to the total pattern of that person's needs and circumstances, and other situations for which it may be merely a form of wishful thinking. As a student once said to me who had read a book based on one such method, "Those positive thinking books all seem to be saying, 'You're better if you think you are,' and I can't believe **that**." She was right, of course, in pinpointing the central assumption underlying most such movements; but the fact remains that some people **are** actually better if they think they are.

Suggestion as Self-Fulfilling Prophecy

The term "self-fulfilling prophecy" refers to any event which actually does happen solely because people believe that it is going to happen. A run on a bank is a good example. If it is widely believed that a certain bank is going to fail, then the depositors rush to take their money out, and the bank actually does fail, not because there was anything necessarily wrong with the bank itself, but because the belief that the bank was going to fail acted as a self-fulfilling prophecy to bring about that very result.

Suggestion may also be viewed as a form of self-fulfilling prophecy. When a hypnotized person is told, for example, "Your right arm is becoming as rigid as an iron bar," the suggestion is accepted and believed in because it has already been accepted that the person is in a state of trance, in which one's mental processes are able to function differently. And, by the same token, if you are able and willing to accept the suggestion that the directed experience which you are about to undergo using the Best Me technique described later in this volume will be one of the most rewarding and fulfilling experiences of your entire life, that's exactly how the experience is going to feel!

Those situations in which suggestion seems to operate most effectively over a long period of time are those in which suggestion tends to act as a self-fulfilling prophecy because it leads to more adaptive long-term patterns of behavior. This is illustrated by an account of a shy, retiring, and painfully self-conscious boy with a large birthmark on his cheek who was able to change his demeanor almost overnight because his grandmother had told him that this birthmark was a special sign from God that he had been singled out as a child destined for greatness. This once forlorn and unhappy lad grew up to lead an adult life full of accomplishment. Clearly, this was an existence which he would probably not have led, were it not for his grandmother's prophecy, which, because it was accepted and believed in, acted to bring about the very conditions which it had predicted.

Suggestion and Consent

As strong as it may be, the power of suggestion is far from absolute. It has long been held, for example, that a hypnotized person cannot be made to do anything which that person would not do in the same situation if he or she were not hypnotized at all. But laboratory experiments designed to investigate whether or not suggestion can make a person engage in anti-social behavior are inherently flawed, because the subjects in these experiments usually respond to the total situation, and not merely to the instructions and suggestions they are given. They know that they have volunteered to be subjects in a psychological experiment, and they believe that no reputable experimenter would really allow them to do anything that would be dangerous to themselves or others. Because of this knowledge, some subjects might go through the motions of complying with whatever they think they are supposed to do, safe in the knowledge that whatever they might **seem** to be doing, they aren't **really** being asked to do anything that would potentially harm themselves or anyone else.

It is often said that the organisms most frequently experimented upon in psychological research are the laboratory rat and the college sophomore, because of their ready availability. But if the results of laboratory research into the power of suggestion are questionable because of the fact that you cannot allow college student volunteers to really violate the norms of society (and they know it!), results from the laboratory of life are more clear cut. For example, I was once asked to testify in a criminal trial involving allegations that hypnosis had been used for anti-social purposes. To support the contention that hypnotized subjects are capable of actions which they would not normally do, the prosecution cited only one instance. Several decades before, in Eastern Europe, a stage hypnotist had handed a hypnotized volunteer from the audience a pistol loaded with blanks, and, stating that the pistol was actually loaded with live ammunition, had commanded the man to shoot him. The volunteer, who was actually an off-duty policeman, drew his service revolver and fired before he could be stopped, wounding several members of the audience.

In my testimony, I pointed out that if it was necessary to go back several decades in time and halfway around the world in order to find even one instance in which hypnosis had been involved in the commission of an anti-social act, it was easier to conclude that the individual in question was mentally deranged than it was to attribute what had happened to the coercive power of hypnosis. Hypnosis has been around in its modern form for over two hundred years; and it is generally agreed that an intelligent person can learn the fundamentals of how to conduct a hypnotic induction in an hour or less. If there were any way to systematically use hypnosis in order to get people to do things against their will, then surely by this time, a way would have been found to do so by thwarted lovers, international espionage agencies, or organized crime, to name just a few possible examples.

Regardless of what is really going on, in the eyes of most people, the use of hypnosis has the effect of shifting the ethical responsibility for what may subsequently transpire completely onto the hypnotist, whereas the actual power in such a situation is primarily in the hands of the subject, in the form of potential legal, professional, and social sanctions which might subsequently be invoked. Indeed, to forestall even the possibility of such allegations being made by unscrupulous or unbalanced subjects who may wish to do so (which can often be as damaging to the professional reputation of the hypnotist as though the alleged misconduct had actually occurred) it is generally desirable to have a third person present or nearby whenever trance suggestions are administered, or else to make a tape recording of the entire proceedings.

Some people occasionally point to the success of cults or totalitarian mass movements as evidence of the coercive power of mass hypnosis. However, such use of the term is far from accurate. When a person uses a political or religious ideology to establish a cult or a mass movement, such an individual may make considerable use of suggestion in the form of propaganda to achieve these ends; and such suggestions may have been carefully chosen with regard to the needs and desires of the intended recipients. In addition, the suggestions may have been administered when the recipients were deliberately placed in a receptive and uncritical frame of mind, as when their emotions were whipped into a frenzy in the course of a political harangue. But if a trance is neither directly suggested nor implied in the suggestions which are given, it is inappropriate to attribute the subsequent influence of such a demagogue to any form of suggestion-induced trance experience. Such effects may be explained much more accurately as an outcome of the demagogue's ability to influence the belief systems of his followers in other ways, and to the ability to control the material and psychological rewards and punishments to which he or she may have access.

2 A Separate Reality

There is an old saying that those who do not know history are doomed to repeat it; and nowhere is this more true than in the history of hypnosis and other forms of trance experiences induced by suggestion. Although various methods for suggesting a change in the perception of one's own awareness have been practiced by witch doctors and medicine men since the dawn of pre-history, modern-day investigations into the nature of these phenomena began with the work of Franz Mesmer, a Viennese physician in the late 1700s, who had become intrigued by an earlier theory that the supposed influence of astrology upon the course of human events lies in the ability of the stars and planets to influence human behavior by means of their magnetic fields. Mesmer decided to test the implications of this theory by getting some magnets and passing them over the bodies of his patients, many of whom were poor peasant folk from the surrounding countryside. The results were startling, to say the least; for in response to this "treatment," many of the patients would promptly go into convulsions, followed by a swoon; and, in addition, they appeared to be cured (at least temporarily) of many ailments which would now be described as hysterical or psychosomatic in nature.

Today, of course, we understand the effects produced by Mesmer as due to the power of suggestion. If stage hypnotists can have highly responsive subjects seeing things that are not really there after only a few words and gestures, it is not surprising that

Mesmer's patients, believing in advance that the "sehr geehrter herr Doktor" was using the tools of science in order to cure them, responded so dramatically to his own ministrations.

Mesmer soon discovered that he could do away with the magnets and produce the same effects merely by means of his gestures alone. Instead of casting about for some other explanation, he simply concluded that the magnetic force was emanating from his own body, and he decided to call his new discovery "animal magnetism." The Viennese medical establishment, however, was not at all impressed by this discovery, and expelled him from their professional society. Mesmer then decided to move to Paris, where, he hoped, post-revolutionary France would be more open to his own brand of revolutionary ideas.

Once established in France, Mesmer had his patients sit along the sides of a large wooden tub, which was filled with a mixture of water, iron filings, and ground glass, with iron rods protruding from holes along its sides, which the patients could then hold on to and apply to the site of their afflictions. Mesmer, dressed in long, flowing robes decorated with the signs of the Zodiac, would walk among them, tapping them with a large wand to speed the healing process still further.

If a piece of iron which is not magnetized is held against a magnet for a while, the non-magnetized iron will become magnetized also. Since both Mesmer and his followers believed that he himself possessed the power of animal magnetism, this analogy with the known properties of magnets was all that was necessary for another suggestion to take effect, i.e., the idea that objects which had been touched by Mesmer would also become magnetized and possess the same power to heal as would a touch from the Master himself. Soon, this was found to be the case; and a brisk demand arose for objects which had been touched by Mesmer, which could be used by his followers without the inconvenience and expense of a visit to the master himself. At the height of the fad, Mesmer "magnetized" an elm tree on the estate of one of his wealthy followers, the Marquis de Puységur, and people would come from miles around to derive the supposed benefits of its wonderful healing powers. One by one, or in small groups, they would stand under the tree until they fell into convulsions, fainted, and were carried away so that others could take their place.

Events were to take yet another turn when a twenty-three year old retarded peasant lad named Victor Emmanuel was brought to stand under the tree. Not knowing what was expected of him, Victor, though he remained standing, fell into a profound slumber. Other patients standing nearby promptly did the same; and this was the forerunner of the modern-day hypnotic trance! It was first manifested by people who were imitating the behavior of a retardate, who was too stupid to know that he was "supposed" to go into convulsions, and went to sleep instead!

It was soon discovered that this "sleeping" response could be directly brought about by suggestion, and that people who were experiencing this mental state would automatically tend to follow any additional suggestions they were given. James Braid coined the term "hypnotism" after the ancient Greek word "hypnos," meaning "sleep," and hypnosis in its modern form was upon us.

As Mesmer had expected, the French government was at least willing to keep an open mind about these events, regardless of how bizarre they may have appeared to be. They appointed a blue-ribbon scientific commission to investigate the phenomena. The commission was chaired Benjamin Franklin, who was the United States ambassador to France at the time, and who had acquired a world-wide reputation as one of the leading scientists of his day. Franklin's committee reached the conclusion that all the phenomena of "animal magnetism" could be explained by imitation and by the workings of the imagination.

Unfortunately, however, the true implications of Franklin's report were long misunderstood. Instead of regarding the imagination as a unique and powerful set of mental abilities, most people tend to think of the word "imaginary" as meaning the opposite of the word "real," with the additional unspoken implication that nothing which has imaginary causes can have real effects. Thus, for many decades, hypnosis was largely left to the province of charlatans and stage entertainers; and it was not until the mid-1950s that so many undeniably real effects of hypnotic treatment were observed that the American Medical Association approved hypnosis as a legitimate area of investigation. Traditionally, however, even though we have long known that hypnosis bears no resemblance to actual sleep, hypnotic procedures still made use of suggestions of relaxation, lethargy, and diminished awareness; and even when they did not, the effects of modeling and imitation were still sufficiently strong that most hypnotized people acted like glassy-eyed zombies.

Today, of course, we know that hypnosis is not a separate, sleep-like state of the organism. In fact, it is possible to suggest that a highly responsive hypnotized person will open his or her eyes and behave as if wide awake, and even an experienced hypnotist is not able to identify the hypnotized subject from among a group of people who are not hypnotized, unless the hypnotist happens to ask, and the hypnotized person is willing to admit the fact.

Just as the outward form of the trance experience is determined by suggestion, phenomena which were previously regarded as objective measures of "trance depth" may now be seen as reactions to expressed or implied suggestions concerning how one is supposed to react to the suggestion that one is hypnotized. Spontaneous amnesia, for example, used to be considered as one measure of how deeply one is "under." But hypnotized people who "normally" do not remember what has occurred during a trance session will do so if it is suggested to them that this will be the case. And some people who respond very well to suggestion and who "normally" do remember everything that has happened while they were hypnotized will not be able to remember these events if it is suggested to them that they will not. Moreover, the "amnesia" which they experience is not a true loss of memory; for if they are hypnotized at a later date and asked to recall the events that they have supposedly forgotten, they are usually able to do so. A modern interpretation is that the ability to not remember (or, more precisely, to act and believe as if one does not remember) is an ability which is possessed by some people who are highly responsive to suggestion.

Today, so many different ways to induce an experience of hypnosis have been developed, such as moving a person's hand back and forth while he stares at it, gazing into the eyes of the hypnotist, etc., that the only thing which they all obviously have in common is plausibly communicating the suggestion that one's conscious processes are beginning to function differently.

The power of suggestion, as I have stated, is rooted in our perception of reality itself. Once a person has accepted the suggestion that his or her conscious processes are functioning differently, if you then suggest, "Now you will get up and walk across the room," this suggestion is likely to be accepted and complied with as just another manifestation of the new reality with which they are now involved. But how can a person who is responding to the suggestion that he or she is hypnotized accept and act upon suggestions which are dramatically different from the reality of everyday life?

Let me answer this question first by means of an example. If I were to ask a volunteer in a hypnosis demonstration to close his or her eyes, and without further ado I suggested, "I'm going to count from one to five, and at the count of five, you will be able to open your eyes and you will see me wearing a Santa Claus suit and hat," the volunteer would surely think that I was crazy. And if such a suggestion should actually happen to work, the volunteer would have thought that he or she was crazy! But if I first suggested eye closure, and then suggested that the volunteer was "going into a deep, sound sleep," and then I had suggested that the volunteer would be able to open his or her eyes at the count of five and see me dressed in a Santa Claus suit, such a suggestion could be accepted and acted upon much more easily because it would be much more credible.

In other words, hypnosis and similar procedures first make use of suggestion to construct a separate reality (often referred to as "trance"), in which a person with a sufficiently skilled imagination, freed from the limitations of everyday logic, is able to convert directly into personal experience whatever additional suggestions he or she is able and willing to comply with.

Is it indeed possible that there may dwell among us a suggestively gifted elite who first need to accept the suggestion that their conscious processes are functioning differently in order for them to be able to exercise certain dramatic powers of the imagination which they carry around with them every day, never even realizing that they have them? In order to understand the unsuspected presence of these abilities in a minority of the general population, let us first consider a phenomenon which is somewhat better understood: the unsuspected **absence** of certain abilities which most of us do possess, namely, color vision.

It is now understood that some people grow up with certain types of color blindness without knowing that their perceptions are different from those around them. The shades of gray which they experience are reinforced with certain names by the verbal community in which they live, and these people simply accept without question that their perceptions are like everyone else's. It is only when they are given a specific test for color blindness, in which certain numbers or letters are embedded in a background of the same brightness, that their color blindness is discovered. By the same token, those who possess uncommon powers of the imagination which are not shared by others in their society are systematically trained to conform to the prevailing world view of the majority; and most of us, beginning in childhood, begin to allow them to wither. Small children are firmly warned not to laugh or cry at the movies, or to become so absorbed in their play that they do not hear their mother's voice calling them in for dinner. Imaginary companions are given up, and the "monsters" in the closet or under the bed are safely exorcized by parental reassurances. As older children and adults, we have to be given permission to resurrect these abilities of the imagination by defining the situation as hypnosis; and some of us may need more specific coaching in order to recover them.

An "induction procedure," then, is not some sort of mechanical process which one person "uses on" another in order to render the latter more compliant with the will of the suggestor, as laymen occasionally tend to perceive it; and neither does it operate in some mysterious manner to open up a direct channel of communication with the "unconscious mind." It is, rather, a method of providing both the opportunity and the rationale for those who are able and willing to utilize their imagination in an "Alice-in-Wonderland" fashion to go ahead and do so. If the active use of the mental abilities loosely referred to as imagination is responsible for what is often referred to as "hypnotic" phenomena, then it is clear to all that the true potential of the human imagination has scarcely been tapped.

Rather than inquiring how many alterations in perceived awareness it is possible to induce by means of suggestion, or how one might go about measuring their reported "depth" (which is, after all, pointless when one is dealing with subjective experiences for which new phenomenological dimensions can be invented, suggested, and consequently experienced by sufficiently responsive subjects virtually at will), it is more appropriate to inquire how such experiences may best be defined and guided to achieve the fullest possible actualization of human potential.

In the early 1970s, I began developing a set of suggestions which I referred to as the **opposite** of hypnosis, because, in contrast to the suggestions of lethargy and diminished awareness which characterized the traditional hypnotic or sleeping induction procedures, these techniques were based on suggestions of mind expansion, increased awareness, and enhanced alertness and sensitivity. In order to minimize the effects of imitation first noted in Franklin's report, it was necessary to clearly differentiate this approach from hypnosis. Following the lead of James Braid, who had coined the term hypnosis from the ancient Greek word for sleep, I chose the ancient Greek word "empiria," or "experience," with the prefix "hyper-" added to denote a greater or an enhanced quality. Hyperempiric inductions and the rationale underlying them were first described in a book entitled *Beyond hypnosis* (Gibbons, 1973). In experimental testing using a standardized test of suggestibility, groups of volunteers who were given either hypnotic or hyperempiric suggestions both demonstrated about an equal increase in responsiveness to suggestion. The results were presented in a paper delivered at the American Psychological Association (Gibbons, 1975), published in a professional journal (Gibbons, 1976), and subsequently expanded into a book entitled *Applied Hypnosis and Hyperempiria* (Gibbons, 1979, 2000). The efficacy of alert inductions was independently verified in a now-classic study by Banyai and Hilgard (1976).

But it is not enough to merely revise the direction and content of an induction if one is going to continue to employ suggestion in more or less conventional ways. After a brief examination of both hypnotic and hyperempiric technique, we will consider a new procedure for scripting suggestions, the Best Me technique, along with illustrations of how this technique may be applied. We will consider these applications in light of both the existing clinical/counseling paradigm and an alternative paradigm in which the dramatic effects produced by suggestion lend themselves to the consideration of human experience itself as the ultimate medium for the creative artist.

3 Preparing for a Trance Experience

In light of the previous discussion, my use of the word "trance" in this volume will refer to a person's involvement with the expressed or implied suggestion that his or her conscious processes are beginning to function differently, which, as we have seen, will vary with both the phenomenological content of the suggestions used, and with the ability and willingness of the participant to comply with them. The physiological accompaniments of trance suggestion are aspects of the mind-body problem and need not concern us here; for our interest lies with the content of such suggestions and with the manner in which they are experienced, as well as with their ultimate purpose and usefulness.

An initial area of concern often centers around doubts about one's own ability to guide another person into trance, or doubts that the process is actually going to work. But you don't have to be a psychologist or possess any special talent in order to be able to use hypnosis or hyperempiria successfully. It is generally agreed that anyone with the "gift of gab" can master the art of trance induction in about an hour or less.

What you say—and how you say it—before the experience begins is just as important as what you say afterwards. By speaking and acting in such a way as to communicate the conviction that the experience is going to be highly effective, the participant begins with an expectation of positive results. For example, in talking about hypnosis or hypererempiria, you shouldn't leave any room for doubt as to whether or not the experience is going to be successful. Say, "when I hypnotize you," or "when you go into hyperempiria," not, "if...."

If the participant should express any doubts as to whether or not the procedure is really going to work, you can reply, "It's all trust and co-operation, and when you co-operate and follow my suggestions, you'll respond just like everyone else does." (which is, indeed, the case.)

Most people become acquainted with the concept of hypnosis as I did, by watching a "monster" movie as a child. Because of the persistence of outmoded, Nineteenth-Century, Svengali-like stereotypes perpetuated by the media, when you are preparing to guide a participant into trance for the first time, it is generally advisable to provide him or her with specific instruction concerning the nature of the experience which they are about to undergo, so that he or she will know what to expect. You might say something like this: "I'm going to ask you to close your eyes and picture some images in your mind, and I'm going to keep talking to you, and as you listen to my voice and continue to picture the images as I describe them, in just a few minutes, you'll be there." It is also helpful to ask if there are any final questions before beginning, so that any remaining doubts and fears have been allayed, and that the experience will be a rewarding and fulfilling one. Many people need to be reassured, for example, that hypnosis or hyperempiria do not render them powerless or make one person dominant over the other, that they will remain fully conscious during the entire procedure, and that they always remain in complete control of the situation because they are just as much themselves after trance suggestions have been given as they were before.

Following is a list of questions which are frequently asked by people who are just learning about trance procedures, and the answers to them. It may be a good idea to discuss many of these questions with the participant, using your own words, even if he or she does not happen to ask specifically about some of the topics mentioned.

What are you going to do? "I will ask you to visualize some pleasant scenes, while I talk about how to use your own mental abilities more effectively. You can always refuse to do anything that you don't want to do, and you can always open your eyes and stop the procedure if you want to, or if an emergency should come up. You will remain completely conscious and aware of what's going on, and you will remember everything that happened when the experience is over."

What does it feel like to be in trance? "The experience of trance is so natural and so commonplace that most of us drift in and out of trance several times a day without realizing it. Any time you let your imagination go and just flow along with a piece of music or a verse of poetry, or lose yourself in watching a sunset or the flickering logs of a fire, or get so involved in watching a movie or a television drama that you feel like you a part of the action instead of a part of the audience, your conscious processes are functioning differently from the way they normally do. Hypnosis and hyperempiria are merely ways of helping you to focus and define this experience, in order to use your mental abilities more freely."

What is the difference between hypnosis, hyperempiria, and a guided fantasy? "In a guided fantasy or visualization exercise, you are simply asked to picture or imagine the scenes which are described. But in hypnosis or hyperempiria, you are able to experience your consciousness in a manner which often lets you become so involved in the experience that it can feel just like everything that is suggested is actually taking place. The difference between hypnosis and hyperempiria is that hypnotic suggestions generally tend to lessen your awareness, and hyperempiric suggestions are intended to increase your awareness. If you want to have the best possible trance experiences, you don't want to feel sleepy or drowsy.

Why can't I just use meditation to accomplish the same thing? "The purpose of a hypnotic or hyperempiric induction is to help you to become more responsive to the suggestions you are given later. But the more you pay attention to your own inner experiences in meditation, the more you tune out everything else!"

Why is suggestion so powerful? "The dramatic power of suggestion lies in allowing you to make the fullest use of your mental abilities, which is why hypnotic suggestion can be used as the sole anesthetic in surgery, and why hyperempiric suggestions leading in the opposite direction (suggestions of mind expansion, increased alertness, and enhanced awareness and sensitivity) are also highly effective."

What can I do to respond better? "Letting go in response to trance suggestions is very similar to letting yourself become absorbed in watching a sunset or the embers of a campfire, or in letting yourself flow with a piece of music or poetry, or feeling like you are part of the action instead of part of the audience when you are watching a movie. People who do not feel that they have been able to respond very well, on the other hand, sometimes find it impossible just to relax in new situations. It all depends on your ability and willingness to go along."

Can you make me do anything I don't want to do? "When you're in trance, you still have your own personality, and you're still **you**, so you won't do anything that you wouldn't do in the very same situation if you were not in trance, and you can easily refuse any suggestion that you don't want to accept. That's why we call them 'suggestions.'"

What if it doesn't work? "As I've said, we all have several changes in conscious experience in the course of a day. The suggestions which lead you into trance merely structure these feelings and define their dimensions, in order to enable you to make the fullest use of the powers of your mind. If you just allow your thoughts to respond freely and naturally to the words and images which lead you into trance, you'll be able to go wherever your mind can take you!"

What if I get so carried away that I don't want to come back? "Sometimes you might not want a movie to end, because the movie is so enjoyable, but you still come back to the real world, because you know it's only a movie. Trance suggestions are basically an exercise for the mind and the imagination, just like a movie script is. But you still come back to everyday life when the session is over, just like you come back at the end of a movie."

If the participant is still doubtful after trance suggestion has been explained, he or she should be encouraged simply to try it. Many people who are able to respond well to suggestion have doubts that the procedure is actually going to work at first, until their natural imaginative abilities become involved enough to show them otherwise.

4 Guiding the Participant into Trance

Whenever you are about to use a particular type of imagery for the first time (going up in a balloon, relaxing on the beach, etc.), if you are not already sure, it is usually a good idea to ask whether or not the participant would feel comfortable with it before you begin. One man, for instance, who was asked to visualize the image of sinking down into a cloud, did not seem to be responding to the hypnotic procedure very well; but when I asked him what was the matter, he was immediately able to tell me, "Well, I'm a pilot, and I can't relax by sinking down into a soft, pink cloud. That means low visibility, and turbulence!"

When you are ready to begin the induction procedure, make sure that the participant is physically comfortable. As soon as you both are ready, you can simply say, "Now, close your eyes," and begin the induction procedure. Suggestions should always be given slowly, in a soothing, gentle tone of voice, stressing a few basic themes designed to engage the imagination, and employing a considerable amount of repetition and redundancy for emphasis, often approaching what would be the point of boredom in an ordinary conversation. It is also often desirable to match the cadence of your spoken suggestions with the rhythm of the participant's breathing, and to vary the speed and length of the procedure to match the ease with which he or she appears to be responding.

If there should be any signs of discomfort during the procedure, permissive instructions and suggestions such as, "It will not disturb you if you need to move or shift your position," may be included. If the discomfort cannot be ended in this manner, the procedure may be smoothly terminated with an appropriate combination of instructions and suggestions such as, "It's all right, you can open your eyes, and any discomfort will quickly pass," or, if the procedure is farther along, by suggesting that the participant's eyes will be open by the count of three, and that he or she will return to an everyday experience of consciousness by that time, and that any remaining discomfort will quickly go away.

On the rare occasions when such discomfort does occur, the participant will usually be able to tell you right away what the difficulty is. Perhaps the imagery, or the wording of a particular suggestion, may suddenly have brought to mind a previous experience which was found to be unpleasant, in which case the procedure may usually be returned to after the appropriate changes in the content of the suggestions have been made.

Sometimes the discomfort may be due to the intrusion of an unpleasant idea, such as the feeling that one is losing control, which results from a faulty understanding of the nature of trance experience. Such misunderstandings are easily dealt with by going back to the relevant information contained in the frequently-asked questions mentioned in the previous chapter. If the participant still does not feel comfortable going on, or if he or she is unable to pinpoint the exact reason for this response even though there is a good understanding of how one is supposed to feel during a trance experience, then of course it is best not to continue until the matter can be cleared up.

Some people are able to open their eyes during a trance without this affecting their altered experience of consciousness. For others, opening one's eyes may simply indicate a momentary confusion. If the participant's eyes should open while you are suggesting a trance experience, it is best to suggest in a matter-of-fact tone of voice, "You can just keep your eyes closed, now, as we go on."

It is important to always remember that whatever you do or say may contribute to defining the trance experience, and therefore function as a suggestion. For example, if you ask in a surprised tone of voice, "Oh, did you come out of it?" with the obvious implication that the participant has done so, then this question may act as a suggestion which will have the effect of canceling the procedure up to that point and making it necessary to start once more from the beginning!

Occasionally, a participant may tend to "get the giggles" during an induction procedure and be unable to continue without bursting out with laughter. Since it is the participant's silence and outward solemnity which seems to trigger such outbursts, it is often best to deal with such situations by adopting a somewhat playful manner yourself, smiling or laughing also and saying something like, "That's all right, this is fun—go ahead and enjoy it!"

The following scripts contain different types of imagery and different types of suggestions to illustrate some of the many ways in which one can guide a participant into trance. They are not intended to be read word for word, although it is possible to do so, if the participant is responsive enough and you read them in a plausible manner, without sounding like you are reading. Generally, however, you should practice your favorite procedure a few times until you truly feel at home with it. Then, once you are familiar enough with the content, you should feel free to change things around to suit the situation, the preferences of the participant, the way in which he or she is able to respond to suggestion, and your own individual style, using whatever imagery and wording may feel most appropriate. There is a considerable amount of freedom in what you are able to do, as long as you keep in mind the basic purpose of such procedures: to convincingly communicate the idea that the participant is undergoing a change in perceived awareness, in order to free the imagination to make the fullest possible use of his or her potential.

5 Hyperempiric Procedures

If you are familiar with the techniques and procedures of traditional hypnosis, you should have no difficulty in utilizing hyperempiria. On the other hand, if your hypnotic technique is a bit "rusty," you may prefer to begin with the hypnotic procedures described in the following chapter. Choose the induction procedure which best suits you, varying the length and content and timing your suggestions to match the participant's responses—or make up your own if you prefer—and, if this is your first time utilizing hyperempiric inductions, get ready for some surprising new experiences!

The Unfolding Flower

"First of all, just sit back or lie down, and make yourself comfortable. And when you are ready, close your eyes.

"Now, with your eyes closed, imagine that it is late on a warm summer night, and that you are peacefully and comfortably resting inside a rosebud which is swaying gently in the soft breeze. If you accept each detail of the scene as I describe it, without trying to think critically, your imagination will be free to allow you to experience the situation just as if you were really there. So just let yourself relax completely now, inside this soft red rosebud, late on a warm summer night. You feel so comfortable resting there, snug and secure and nestled down among the petals of the flower.

"You can feel the soft summer breeze gently caressing the outside of the bud. Just keep listening to the breeze outside, and continue to focus on the beauty and the peacefulness which is all around you. And as you continue to allow yourself to be guided by my voice, I am going to show you how to release your awareness for its fullest possible functioning.

"There is a rustle of wind through the leaves. And as the soft, red petals around you gently begin to stir, you can feel the breeze beginning to filter through to you as the bud prepares to open. Let yourself breathe slowly and deeply now, as you inhale the warm night air and your consciousness commences to expand and unfold along with the flower.

"The late night air is so pure, so fresh, and so crystal clear. Feel it entering your lungs, and feel the warmth of it entering your body as your awareness continues to expand. In....out...in...out.

"As the bud begins to open, you look up and see that the sky is strewn with hundreds of blinking, bluish-white stars. And as the bud expands more and more, your awareness is unfolding along with it, as you continue breathing slowly, in....and out, in....and out....carrying this expanding awareness to every part of your body.

"The rose petals are releasing a delicate perfume as the bud opens wider. Breathe in this joyous scent and follow its passage from your nostrils into your lungs. Let yourself become ever more aware of the rhythm of your breathing, as it carries you on to ever increasing sensations of awareness. With every breath you take, your consciousness drifts higher. With every breath you take, your awareness is expanding, and your capacity for experience is becoming exquisitely greater.

"The rose petals are expanding more rapidly now, and the bud is nearly open. As the bud continues to unfold, your feelings of joy and exaltation continue to expand along with it. You can feel your awareness continuing to grow, and your capacity for experience becoming greater and more intense than anything you have known before.

"Now the blossom is fully open. The petals are extended as far as they will go, and your awareness also is in full flower. And while you remain within hyperempiria, every sensation and everything you experience will be intensely pleasurable, and each of these new experiences will be greater and more profound than you ever thought possible."

On the Beach at Night

"Just relax now, and close your eyes. Imagine that it is late at night, and that you are lying on a sandy beach, late on a warm spring evening. Just keep your eyes closed and let yourself relax completely on that sandy beach, as you feel the gentle breeze blowing from the direction of the ocean, and savor the freshness of the salty night air.

"As you listen to the sound of the waves gently breaking upon the shore, you can just let yourself go and relax completely.

"There is a bright, starlit sky overhead, broken here and there by patches of dark, gray clouds and an occasional shaft of moonlight. Now, as you continue to allow yourself to be guided by my voice, I am going to show you how to expand your awareness, letting it rise to a much higher level than you have known previously.

"You are beginning to experience an intense feeling of awareness now. And with each passing second, your mind becomes more sensitive and more responsive. And with each passing second, the more pleasant and the more beautiful the scene around you becomes.

"It's a wonderful feeling of liberation which you are experiencing now, as all of your vast, untapped potentials are becoming freed for their fullest possible functioning.

"The beauty and the joy of the scene around you continues to increase, as you feel your consciousness expanding, more, and more, and more. And the more your awareness increases, the more beautiful it all becomes; for your capacity for awareness and your capacity for experience is becoming infinitely greater than it could be at any other time.

"Now, you are beginning to enter fully into hyperempiria. Soon, all of your senses will be tuned to their highest possible pitch, and your entire capacity for experience will be greater than it ever was before. Your perceptions will be keener; and you will discover new and greater experiences, which will be more intense and more exciting than any which you have ever known before."

The Balloon Ride

"Now, with your eyes closed, imagine that you are sitting or lying inside the basket of a large balloon. If you accept each detail of the scene as I describe it, your imagination will be free to allow yourself to experience the situation just as if you were really there. So just let yourself relax now, in that large wicker basket, while the balloon above you slowly begins to fill.

"It is a beautiful spring day. You can smell the sweet, fresh air of the surrounding meadow, laden with the gentle fragrance of wild flowers. You can hear the soft rustling of the grass around the basket, and the song of birds in the distance. As you feel the gentle breeze upon your face and the warm sun upon your skin, the balloon will begin to rise. And the higher you go, the greater your awareness will become.

"I'm going to count from one to ten, and at the count of one the balloon will begin to rise. And with each count it will go higher. As it does, you will feel your awareness expanding along with it, until you will feel as if you are able to hold within your own consciousness an awareness of the entire Universe, and all its beauty.

"Now the balloon is nearly full. And as it begins to rise, I will begin to count, as your consciousness commences to expand.

"One. As the balloon slowly begins to rise, you are beginning to enter a new and different experience of awareness. You will find that you begin to experience very pleasant feelings of increased sensitivity.

"Two. You are beginning to enter a higher level now, as your awareness becomes more sensitive and more responsive with every word that I utter.

"Three. As the balloon continues to rise, you can feel the basket gently swaying in the breeze, rocking you back and forth as it does, and you can hear the sound of the wind blowing in gentle bursts as you continue to float up and up.

"Four. Your perceptions are becoming keener as you float on, higher and higher. It's such a pleasant feeling as you drift on, and on, and as your awareness expands more, and more, and more.

"Five. As you continue to rise higher and higher, you can feel the balloon swaying and turning in the breeze, as you drift on, high above the earth. And the higher you go, the higher you want to go, and the higher you go, the higher you are able to go, and the stronger the effects of my words become.

"Six. As you feel your consciousness expanding more and more, you are experiencing an ever-growing sense of joy, as all of your senses are being tuned to their highest possible pitch.

"Seven. It's a wonderful feeling of liberation which you are experiencing now, as all of your potentials for experience are being tuned to their highest possible functioning. And by the time I get to the count of ten, you will have reached the peak of your potential. Your perceptions of the world around you will take on new and deeper qualities, and they will possess a greater depth of reality than anything you have experienced previously.

"Eight. You can feel yourself drifting up, into the sky now, hanging on the very edge of space. Soon you will be able to travel on by yourself, into new dimensions of experience, with only my voice to guide you. As the balloon continues to rise, your feeling of joy continues to increase as you feel your capacity for experience becoming infinitely keener.

"Nine. All the way up into the sky now, and ready to travel on into new dimensions of awareness.

"Ten. Now, you are ready. And while you remain in hyperempiria, all your perceptions will be much more profound as we explore new experiences together. Your experiences will be more intense, and more exciting than you have ever had before, leaving you with a sense of total enjoyment."

Riding Through a Rainbow

"Now, with your eyes closed, picture yourself floating high above the earth, drifting, and dreaming, and floating through patches of fleecy white clouds, just after a sudden spring shower. If you accept each detail of the scene as I describe it, without trying to think critically, your imagination will be free to allow you to experience the situation just as if you were really there.

"Feel yourself drifting on now, as you continue to listen to my voice. Drifting slowly and gently, on and on, until you come to a beautiful rainbow, shimmering brightly before you, with shades of hearty red, creamy peach, golden yellow, cool mint green, aqua blue, and dusky violet.

"You think how pleasant it would be to drift on through the rainbow, experiencing the colors one by one. And changing direction ever so slightly, you prepare to do just that, starting first with the band of hearty red.

"Feel the band of red beginning to enter the soles of your feet now, carrying with it a warm glow of strength and power which spreads quickly up through the calves of your legs, and on up through the rest of your body, flooding every fiber and nerve with a warm, rosy glow of energy and strength and power. Let yourself breathe deeply and slowly, as you continue on through the band of red, and inhale the color and the feelings that go with it. Let yourself experience them fully and completely, as you breathe them in and saturate yourself in their warmth.

"Now, as you continue slowly drifting on, the band of creamy peach begins to penetrate the soles of your feet and spreads itself throughout your body in just the same way as did the red, bringing with it an indescribably beautiful sensation of complete and perfect peace. And as this peacefulness progresses on throughout your body, it blends with the energy which you already feel, making you serenely more aware of everything you experience.

"Next, the golden yellow band begins to spread itself throughout your being, filling and flooding you with its delicious golden glow, and bringing to your consciousness an ever-increasing sense of happiness and well-being. Flow with it and breathe it in, as you allow yourself to merge completely with this wave of radiant happiness, blending with it so completely that you begin to radiate back an answering happiness of your own.

"You are entering the green band now, as you begin to experience a wave of pure, refreshing joy, carrying you ever higher, as you feel yourself being inundated by endless sensations of indescribably joy and bliss. Rapture and ecstasy, wonder and delight....Breathe it in, blend with it, and savor the delicious emotions which are being added now to all of the other feelings you have gathered in your journey through the rainbow, and which you still retain.

"Now you are beginning to draw in the color of aqua blue, which causes you to feel as free and as fluid as the aqua waters themselves. Feel yourself blending, in your imagination, with all the water everywhere on the planet, rushing over the surface of the earth as her banks caress you, moving over rocks and soft river beds, plunging down cliffs to form waterfalls in a headlong rush to the sea, where you are again drawn up to the sky and back to the rainbow and the blue band once more, ready to enter the next band of light, but retaining this sensation of freedom which becomes blended with all the others.

"Finally, you enter the violet band on the inner side of the rainbow. It fills you silently as nightfall, extending your previous feelings of freedom to an almost infinite degree; for you now feel able to step behind all your everyday thoughts and all your customary social roles.

"You slowly drift to a stop within this violet band, and you are filled with the stillness and peace of a warm, mimosa-scented summer night. You can feel within your own being the beautiful, tranquil color of the violet sky, long after the sun has slipped down behind the horizon. And while you remain here within this violet band of light, in the hyperempiric trance which you have entered, the suggestions which you receive will help to guide you into new paths of awareness and new dimensions of being, richer and more rewarding than those you have known before."

The Cathedral of the Mind

"Just make yourself comfortable and close your eyes; and I am going to show you how to release your consciousness, so that it may rise to a higher level than you have known previously.

"First of all, I would like you to picture yourself standing in front of two large wooden doors, which are the doors to a great cathedral. This cathedral represents the cathedral of your mind, which contains the highest, most solemn, and most sacred reservoir of your potential for personal and spiritual growth. If you accept each detail of the scene as I describe it, without trying to think critically, your imagination will be free to allow you to experience the situation just as if you were really there. Just let yourself stand there a few seconds, gazing at the carved wooden panels of the door as you prepare to enter.....

"Soon the doors will open and you will go inside, as I guide you into a higher state of awareness called hyperempiria. You will begin to experience very pleasant feelings of increased alertness and sensitivity as your consciousness commences to expand.

"As the doors swing open and you enter the cathedral, you first traverse a small area paved with stone and stop at the font, if you desire. Then you pause before a second pair of doors which leads to the interior. You are beginning to enter a higher level of consciousness now, for this cathedral provides you with an image which will allow your consciousness to encompass all of the vast reservoirs of strength and spiritual power contained within your own being, and within the Universe as well. And as you enter, you can begin to feel all these vast resources flowing into your own awareness.

"As you pass through the second pair of doors and into the dimly lit interior, you can hear gentle tones of music floating on the quiet air. Let yourself breathe slowly and deeply now, as you inhale the faint aroma of incense, and your consciousness drifts higher.

"Breathe slowly and deeply, as you inhale the incense and listen to the music. Feel it flowing through you, and filling the very core of your being. let your mind flow with it. Let the music merge completely with your own awareness and carry it along. And soon you will feel as if you are able to hold within your own consciousness an awareness of the entire Universe, and all its beauty.

"You are entering into a much higher level of consciousness now, one in which your ability to utilize your full capacity for experience is greatly enhanced. You can feel a pleasant exaltation in your ability to use your imagination so much more effectively, as your awareness continues to expand, more, and more, and more.

"Your perceptual abilities are becoming infinitely keener, as the music swells within you; yet you can still direct your attention, as you would normally, to anything you wish. It's such a pleasant feeling, as your awareness expands, more and more, multiplying itself over and over again.

"It's a wonderful feeling of release and liberation which you are experiencing now, as all of your vast, untapped potentials are being freed for their fullest possible functioning. And in just a short while, your entire potential for awareness and for experience will be fully realized. Your perceptions of the world around you will take on new and deeper qualities, and they will contain a greater depth of reality than anything you could have experienced previously.

"Some distance away from you stands the High Altar, bordered by banks of softly glowing candles. As the music continues, and your awareness continues to grow, you can feel yourself being drawn irresistibly toward it. And as you approach, the closer you get, the more your awareness expands, and the more pleasant it becomes.

"As you feel your consciousness expanding more and more, you can feel an ever-growing sense of joy as all of your abilities are being tuned to their highest possible pitch, and it's not fatiguing or tiring in the least.

"As you approach nearer and nearer to the High Altar, you can feel your awareness and your capacity for experience becoming infinitely greater than it could possibly be in any other state. In just a few seconds now, all your mental abilities will be tuned to their highest possible pitch; and you will be able to concentrate much, much better than you can in an ordinary state of consciousness.

"Now, you are ready. All of the vast resources within you have been freed for their fullest possible functioning; and while you remain within this state of hyperempiria, you will be able to discern new and greater levels of reality, new realms of meaning, and new dimensions of experience, greater and more profound than anything you have encountered previously."

The Enchanted Cottage

The following hyperempiric procedure was originally conceived as an induction for children. Because of their normally short attention span (except when they are spellbound listening to a story or a fairy tale!) I believed that an induction centered around a fairy tale format would be desirable for children of grade school age and younger. Although these assumptions proved to be correct, I was more than a little surprised when some students in my graduate-level classes in hypnosis and hyperempiria often told me that they also found this induction to be one of their favorites. Only then did I realize that because the essence of an induction procedure *is* to facilitate the transition from the practical world of everyday reality into a more accepting, childlike frame of mind, it should not have been surprising at all that an induction procedure centered around a fairy tale theme should be particularly effective in letting one's inner child out to play, regardless of one's calendar age.

"Lie back now and close your eyes, and I am going to tell you a magic story. It is a story about a very special place, deep in an enchanted forest, where everything I tell you will come true. And it is a magic story because, if you listen carefully and believe hard enough, it will really take us there. So listen carefully to what I have to say, and soon we will be on our way to that very special place, deep in the magic forest, where everything I tell you will come true.

"Imagine now that we are walking together down a long, winding path which runs through the middle of a large woods. We are walking together hand in hand, early on a bright spring morning. Birds are singing in the trees, and here and there a flower is poking its head out of the soft, green grass which grows beside the path. And because this is a magic story, the farther we go along the path, the more real everything around us becomes.

"Now and then a ray of sunlight makes its way down through the branches of the trees and falls upon the dewdrops in the grass, causing them to sparkle like a million tiny diamonds. The air is fresh and cool, with gentle breezes blowing now and then, causing the trees, and the grass, and the flowers to move ever so slightly as if everything in the world were feeling so happy on this bright spring morning that nothing could keep still for very long.

"And because this is a magic story, the farther we go along the path, the more real everything becomes.

"As we continue on our walk, we can begin to be aware of the sound of rushing water. With each passing second, the sound is becoming clearer and clearer still.

Suddenly, we find ourselves standing beside the bank of a forest stream, which is the source of the sound we have been hearing. The water is flowing past us swift and clear, for it has come tumbling down from a magic spring many miles away in the hills. And because the water from the magic spring is enchanted, everyone who drinks it will be enchanted, too. And when we drink from the water of the enchanted stream, we will easily be able to find that special place, deep in the magic forest, where everything I tell you will come true.

"We dip our hands eagerly into the bubbling stream and cup them together, bringing the cool, fresh water up to our lips again and again, until we have taken all we want.

"Now it is time to hurry on our way once more; for the water from the magic spring has made it certain that we will soon find that very special place in the enchanted forest, where everything I tell you will come true; and we know now that it cannot be far away.

"As we continue on our journey, we notice a tiny path leading off to one side, and we decide to go up this path to see where it leads. Before very long, we notice that the woods are beginning to thin out, and that we are about to enter a clearing. And as we approach nearer and nearer to the edge of the clearing, we can see that the path we have been following leads right up to a small cottage.

"This is that very special place I have been telling you about, where everything will come true. For as long as we stay here, in this enchanted cottage, in the enchanted forest, even my words will be enchanted, and everything I tell you will really happen exactly as I say it will.

"The door to the enchanted cottage is standing slightly open as we hurry up the path, and as soon as we reach the entrance we hurry on inside in order to lose no more time.

"We have arrived now, at that very special enchanted place in the enchanted forest which we have traveled so far to reach. And as long as we remain here, in this enchanted cottage, everything I say and everything I describe to you will come true as soon as I have said it. For as long as we remain here, in this enchanted place, even my words will be enchanted."

Heightening the Experience of Hyperempiria

Regardless of which set of suggestions you have used to guide the participant into hyperempiria, the following suggestions can be added to focus the experience and to help to give your participant an increased involvement with your trance suggestions..

"You are continuing to go higher and higher into hyperempiria with every word that I utter. And as you feel yourself carried on to ever greater heights, the higher you go, the stronger and the more pronounced the effects of my words become. The higher you go, the more easily you are able to respond to everything I say, and the clearer and the sharper are the results.

"As you continue to be guided ever higher by my voice, you can experience everything that is suggested to you just as if it is actually happening. And as you continue soaring higher and higher into hyperempiria, your ability to directly experience the reality of whatever is suggested to you will be a never ending source of wonder and delight....wonder and delight."

6 *Hypnotic Gateway into Hyperempiria*

Some people who may have been hypnotized before, or who may have become accustomed to meditation or other procedures centered around relaxation, may find it initially easier to adapt to hyperempiria by first going down into hypnosis, and then up into hyperempiria. Still others, who may initially be inclined to be a bit apprehensive, may find it helpful to first utilize a relaxation-based approach. By the same token, therapists who have become familiar with more traditional approaches may also find it more comfortable to start with those procedures to which they have already become accustomed, using them as a base from which they can then easily guide the participant up into hyperempiria. Later, as the participant begins to utilize the procedures described in the instructions for rapid re-entry into hyperempiria, these preliminaries can usually be done away with. Your own and the participant's personal preferences are usually the best guide to the procedures that will be most effective and the easiest to employ.

As is the case with hyperempiric techniques, if the participant should express any particular preferences or reservations concerning the use of specific imagery (for example, if it is difficult for the participant to relax while imagining that one is floating on a rubber raft because he or she happens to have a fear of water or is a non-swimmer), other imagery may easily be substituted, such as relaxing on a grassy bank beside a mountain stream, or sinking down in a soft feather bed. If, on the other hand, the participant indicates that there would be no difficulty in utilizing such imagery, you may proceed in a manner similar to the following:

"First of all, just close your eyes and imagine that it's a warm summer's day, and that you're floating around on a soft rubber raft at the beach, just beyond the breakers, and a couple of hundred feet from shore. Just picture the scene and imagine yourself resting there on that soft rubber raft, with the water gently rocking you back and forth, as you enjoy the sunlight and the cool ocean breeze. It's so calm and so peaceful out there, with the sound of the water breaking nearby, that all you want to do is to just keep drifting and dreaming, and floating on, and on, and on into a deep, peaceful, and refreshing hypnotic sleep. Just continue to picture the scene as I describe it, while I count slowly from one to ten; and by the time I get to the count of ten, you will be resting comfortably in a deep, sound, peaceful sleep..

"One. You can feel yourself relaxing now, relaxing so very, very deeply, as you continue floating on and on, with the water gently rocking you and the sunlight flooding your body with its soft, golden warmth.

"Two. You can feel a heavy, relaxed feeling coming over you as you continue to listen to my voice. You can feel your arms relaxing, and your legs relaxing, and your entire body relaxing completely, as you continue floating, on and on, into a deep, peaceful and relaxing sleep.

"Three. You can feel yourself relaxing even more deeply now, as that heavy, relaxed feeling continues to grow. You are relaxing deeper and deeper all the time, as you continue to drift and to float, slowly and gently, on, and on, and on.

"Four. You can feel that heavy, relaxed feeling growing stronger and stronger. And as I continue the count on up to ten, that heavy, relaxed feeling is going to continue growing stronger with every passing second, until it causes you to drift into a deep, sound sleep.

"Five. Every word that I utter is putting you into a deep, sound sleep, as I continue to count and that heavy, relaxed feeling continues to grow. You are relaxing so very, very deeply now, relaxing so deeply that you can just let yourself go completely and begin to drift even faster into a deep, sound sleep.

"Six. Just listen to my voice, as I continue to count, and by the time I get to the count of ten, you will be resting comfortably in a deep, sound sleep.

"Seven. You are drifting even faster now, drifting faster and faster into a deep, sound sleep; and by the time I get to the count of ten, you will be resting comfortably in a deep, sound sleep.

"Eight. Every word that I utter is putting you faster and faster into a deep, sound sleep, deeper and faster, and deeper and faster, all the time. You are drifting very, very rapidly now into a deep, sound sleep, a deep, sound sleep.

"Nine. Into a deep, sound sleep now, a deep, sound sleep.

"Ten. Very deeply drifting, in a deep, sound sleep. Very deeply drifting, in a deep, sound sleep. Continuing to drift deeper, with each passing second, drifting deeper and deeper, down, and down, and down."

Hypnosis with Kinesthetic Imagery

The following technique is particularly helpful for those who may have difficulty with visual images. It also provides you with excellent feedback concerning the participant's responsiveness, as indicated by the ease and rapidity with which his or her arm descends and then rises in response to suggestion, allowing you to adjust the length of the procedure fairly easily. You can also spot resistance, as revealed by the inclination to maintain one's arm in a relatively stationary position, or even to move it in the opposite direction to the one which you suggest. With appropriate allowances for variation in individual responsiveness, suggestions may be given as follows:

"Just close your eyes now, and listen to my voice. I would like you to hold your right [or left] arm straight out in front of you, with the palm facing upward. That's right: arm straight out in the air in front of you, with the palm facing upward. Now, just imagine that you are holding an empty bucket in that hand, and that I'm slowly pouring some sand into the bucket. And as I do, you will feel your arm getting heavier and heavier as the bucket pulls it down more and more. As it does, it will pull you deeper and deeper into hypnosis. And as soon as your arm touches your lap, or touches the chair, you will instantly go into a very deep hypnotic sleep.

"Now I've poured five pounds of sand into the bucket, and you can feel it pulling your arm down, pulling your arm down, more and more, and pulling you into hypnosis. Your arm is beginning to sink down more and more now, as you feel the weight of the bucket pulling it down, and down....Seven pounds, and your arm is sinking down and down. Your arm is sinking down more and more as I continue pouring sand into the bucket; and as it does, it's pulling you deeper and deeper into hypnosis. Ten pounds....Fifteen pounds....In just a few seconds now, your arm will touch your lap or touch the arm of the chair, and you will instantly go into a deep, hypnotic sleep, a much deeper sleep than you have ever been in before. Reach to touch....Ready to touch. Ready to touch....**Now**.

"You are continuing to sink deeper and deeper into hypnosis with every word that I utter. And as you continue drifting down and down into a very deep, hypnotic sleep, I would like you to visualize a large balloon, which is fastened to your other wrist by means of a string. As I continue to speak, the balloon is going to begin pulling this arm up, until it is extended straight out in the air in front of you.

"You can feel this arm becoming lighter now, as I continue to speak; and you can feel the balloon beginning to pull on it.

"Your arm is beginning to rise up into the air now, rising up and up. It is rising faster and faster now. Continuing to rise, up and up, continuing to go higher. In just a few seconds, your arm will be straight out in front of you, and then I will touch it. As I do, it will drop down into a normal resting position as I cut the string which holds the balloon, and you will instantly go much deeper into hypnosis

"Your arm is almost straight out in front of you, and I am going to touch it as I cut the string which is holding it to the balloon; and as soon as I do so, your arm will drop back into a normal resting position, and you will instantly go much deeper into hypnosis than you are right now. Ready? **Now.**"

Intensifying the Trance Experience

What is commonly referred to as "taking a person deeper into hypnosis," or "higher into hyperempiria," is actually any method of increasing the credibility and the degree of one's imaginative involvement with the suggested trance experience. Thus, the suggestions for heightening the experience of hyperempiria which were discussed previously may easily be modified with slight changes in wording to provide suggestions for intensifying the experience of hypnosis. Another deepening procedure (which, of course, can also be modified to be used as a hypnotic induction) is as follows:

"Now, I'm going to count from one to twenty; and by the time I get to the count of twenty, you will be much more deeply hypnotized than you are right now. Just imagine that you are at the top of a long staircase which has twenty steps, and picture yourself getting ready to go down the stairs one by one as I begin to count.

"With each count, you will descend, one step at a time. And with each step that you descend, you will go one step deeper into hypnosis. One. Going deeper now, just let yourself sink deeper into hypnosis, as you descend the first step. Two. Going down another step, and continuing to go deeper as you do. Three. Going deeper yet, as you continue to descend. By the time I get to the count of twenty, you will be deeper than ever before. Four. You descend the fourth step now, and you go still deeper. Five. The fifth step, and you continue going **much deeper** into hypnosis with every step you take.

"Now I'm going to let you continue on down the staircase by yourself, all the way to the twentieth step at the bottom. Just let yourself keep going down the staircase, counting out loud with each step, as you continue to descend all the way to the bottom. Now you can begin to count out loud, and continue counting all the way down."

Some people who may be inclined to be rather passive may need to be reminded once or twice to begin to count out loud, or to continue counting all the way up to twenty. As the participant begins to count, it is helpful to intersperse suggestions such as the following at appropriate intervals:

"Going on by yourself now, all the way to the twentieth step at the bottom, and in just a moment or two, you will have reached the bottom of the stairs, and you will be in a **very** deep hypnotic trance. Just continue to count out loud, as you continue to descend the staircase, and in a moment or so, you will have reached the bottom."

The foregoing suggestions may be modified to heighten a suggested hyperempiric experience (or, with the appropriate suggestions, used as a hyperempiric induction) by asking the participant to picture himself/herself standing at the **foot** of a staircase leading **upward**, and suggesting that with each count, he or she will ascend one step, and that as this happens, the participant will go higher.

Time Expansion

All too frequently, pleasant experiences seem to be over in just a short while, regardless of how long they have actually lasted, and events which are perceived as dull or boring find us with time hanging on our hands. However, the subjective sense of the passage of time may easily be altered by means of suggestion (Cooper, 1956; Cooper & Erickson, 1954), thus permitting this effect to be nullified or even reversed.

Suggestions of time expansion may be utilized in conjunction with a trance induction technique in order to enhance the experiential qualities of other suggestions, potentially increasing both their desirability and their effectiveness. At the conclusion of a hyperempiric or a hypnotic induction, suggestions may be provided as follows:

"During the remainder of your trance experience, time will seem to be passing very, very slowly for you. It's going to seem as if your trance experience will be going on for a much, much longer time than it actually is. And because time will seem to be passing so slowly, your enjoyment of the experience, and all of the other benefits which you will derive from it, will be correspondingly increased. Then, when the trance experience is over, your normal sense of the passage of time will be restored also."

7 Self-Induced Trance Experiences

The possibility of administering trance suggestions to oneself may occasionally strike some people as being a bit farfetched. Yet, many persons spontaneously discover ways of using autosuggestion in everyday life without actually being aware that they are doing so. It is by no means uncommon, for example, to be able to awaken oneself regularly at the same time each morning without an alarm clock, with due allowance for the changing seasons made without apparent effort, or to change the time during which one regularly does awaken, merely by making an appropriate resolution to oneself the previous night. Many people are also able to "talk themselves into" carrying out household chores when they are not initially in the proper mood for such activities; or they may have learned how to cheer themselves up by thinking pleasant thoughts or "whistling a happy tune" when they are temporarily depressed or fearful.

Provided one is sufficiently responsive to suggestion, the ability to suggest a trance experience to oneself is largely a matter of willingness, practice, and confidence; and the necessary confidence is most easily acquired by having another person administer the initial inductions and turn the responsibility over to the participant in a few successive stages.

After a hypnotic or hyperempiric induction has been administered in the usual manner, the therapist may proceed as follows:

"Now I'm going to show you how to give yourself a suggestion, and how to terminate the trance by yourself as well. First of all, I'd like you to think of something that you can tell yourself to do right after the trance is over. It might be a suggestion to yourself that you will touch your right ear, or that you will stand up and shake hands, or reach down tie your shoe, or almost anything else that you can think of; but whatever it is, it should be something that you can do within a minute or two after the trance is over.

"When you have decided what it is that you are going to do, you will only have to think to yourself the suggestion, 'After I come out of the trance, I will do such, and such,' and you will be able to carry out whatever suggestion you have given yourself just as well and just as effectively as if I had given the suggestion to you.

"Then, when you are ready to bring yourself out of the trance, you will be able to do so by silently counting from one to five and telling yourself as you do that you are gradually coming back, more and more, and that by the time you get to the count of five you will be all the way back, feeling wonderful. Of course, you won't have to use my exact words, just whatever words feel right and natural to you as you bring yourself out of the trance by thinking these suggestions silently to yourself.

"And later on, you will be able to carry out the entire process by yourself: you will be able to place yourself in trance by sitting back and closing your eyes and silently counting from one to ten, using whatever imagery and whatever words you find comfortable and convenient, telling yourself that by the time you get to the count of ten you will be in a trance; and then you can give yourself a post-trance suggestion and bring yourself out in the manner that I have just described. You will always be able to hear and to respond to any outside stimuli, and you will be able to bring yourself out of the trance very easily and very rapidly any time the need should arise.

"But right now, just go ahead and give yourself a suggestion that you are going to do something right after the trance is over, and then bring yourself out as soon as you are ready."

If the participant appears to be taking an unduly long time, it may occasionally be necessary to prompt him or her with a few suggestions couched as reassuring observations: "Almost ready to open your eyes now, feeling just fine," or, "Soon your eyes will be open and the trance will be over, and you're going to be feeling absolutely wonderful."

If the participant carries out his or her previously administered autosuggestion within a reasonable time after their eyes have opened, they are ready to attempt the entire procedure by themselves: to suggest a trance, administer additional autosuggestions, and to bring themselves out of trance as soon as they are ready. Most responsive participants are eager to try out their newly acquired abilities immediately; and it usually helpful for them to do so, if they wish, within a few moments after the previous trance experience has been terminated and while the instructor is still present. However, some participants may refer to attempt their first autoinduction at home or in some other setting where they will be able to schedule an abundance of time to themselves, free of distractions and outside interference—perhaps just before they go to sleep at night. This latter alternative is especially preferable in those cases in which a participant's initial responses to autosuggestion have been weak or uncertain.

Many instructors like to encourage participants to word autosuggestions in the first person: "My whole body feels calm and relaxed," etc. Alternatively, the participant may be instructed to address himself or herself in a totally objective manner, as if it were an outside observer giving the suggestions: "Feel your whole body relaxing now, deeper and deeper." I personally believe that it makes little difference how autosuggestions are worded as long as one understands that in order for an autosuggestion to be whole-heartedly accepted and believed (even with the aid of trance suggestion) it must be wholeheartedly believed **in**. Only when the participant is able and willing to unreservedly believe in the essential goodness, rightness, and appropriateness of a given autosuggestion for his or her own life can autosuggestions fulfill their true potential. Indeed, in the absence of such underlying beliefs, it is difficult to escape the feeling that one is merely lying to oneself.

In general, all participants should be cautioned to check with a qualified professional before attempting to employ these skills for any purpose other than that for which they have initially been taught. Occasionally, for example, a participant might be inclined to use autosuggestion to block out recurring sensations of pain after aspirin and other over-the-counter analgesics have proved ineffective, only to discover (perhaps when it is too late) that one should have consulted a physician as soon as the discomfort began.

It is also desirable to discourage the use of self-induced trance techniques by cultists who wish to "re-experience past lifetimes," or perhaps "learn astral projection." Such people are often unable to comprehend that it is just as easy to suggest that one is a cabbage as a king; and depending on the ability of the participant to visualize and live out such suggestions, both will be experienced as equally "real." But a suggested hallucination is still an hallucination, regardless of whether or not it happens to coincide with one's occult beliefs, and is simply a demonstration of the ease with which even the most absurd imaginings can be momentarily experienced as though they were actually true.

Although there is little likelihood of individuals with psychotic tendencies using self-induced trance experiences to develop a Jekyll-and-Hyde personality, it is probably not advisable to encourage the use of autosuggestion by those who are obviously psychotic or pre-psychotic, since such people are generally not able to use these techniques appropriately. However, trance sessions conducted by skilled therapists have been successfully employed to assist such individuals.

8 Three Things to Remember—And One to Forget

Many people who have been trained in the use of trance suggestion still do not feel comfortable in using it. Most workshops operate under strict time limitations; and since the results of a demonstration of trance phenomena are often so dramatic, many people leave these workshops with lingering doubts about their own ability to replicate what they have just seen, with many unanswered questions about what they saw taking place.

If you or some of your colleagues are among those many individuals who have had such training but rarely if ever use it, I would like to offer you three things to remember, and one to forget.

First, *remember that the ability to respond to suggestion follows the normal, bell-shaped curve,* with some people on the high end, some people on the low end, and most people bunched up somewhere in between. In any large group, there are enough high responders who are willing to volunteer that stage hypnotists have no trouble dazzling the rest of the audience with the dramatic effects which are produced merely by suggesting that they are going to happen. But it has now been demonstrated that with the proper coaching and instruction, individuals may learn to become absorbed in the fantasy and selective inattention of hypnosis in much the same manner that they once became absorbed in the fantasy and selective inattention of children's play (Gorassini & Spanos, 1999).

Second, remember that the long-term effectiveness of your suggestions has nothing to do with your client's experience of trance, or their degree of involvement with the suggestion that his or her conscious processes are beginning to function differently. Trance suggestions, as we have seen, provide a rationale to facilitate the acceptance of suggestions which are given after the induction procedure has been completed. But in order to explain why some of these suggestions are accepted and retained over time while others are not, we need to remember one more thing:

Third, remember that a participant is responding to the total situation, and not just to your suggestions. I once hypnotized a co-worker who wanted to stop smoking. She told me that she usually smoked five to ten cigarettes per day. After the induction, I provided what I considered to be appropriate suggestions about the benefits and rewards of smoking versus non-smoking. The next day, I was horrified when she told me, "I went home, took a pack of cigarettes, and smoked them all up in less than an hour." Six months later, I made a casual reference to her smoking, and she replied, "Oh, I haven't had a cigarette in six months now." Greatly surprised, I said nothing. But, knowing her as well as I and the other members of our department did, I soon realized that the reason she had initially acted in such a contrary manner was that one of the rules by which she lived was, "Nobody's going to tell ME what to do!" She had arrived at a place in her life where she was ready to quit smoking; and being hypnotized provided the proper occasion for her to implement this decision; but only **after** her existing beliefs about personal autonomy had been satisfactorily expressed.

With these three things to remember, if the thought should still come to mind that you are just "not any good" at using suggestion to bring about trance experiences, **forget it!** Of course, by chance alone, you could always encounter three or four people in a row who happen to be on the low end of the bell-shaped curve of suggestibility. But If you define hypnosis for your clients in a manner which is within their experiential repertoire, and if you obtain sufficient ongoing feedback to appropriately modify and re-direct your suggestions in terms of their existing needs and belief structures, your task as your clients make the cognitive shift from our everyday, logic-driven mode of experience to the freer, more imaginative and accepting style which is characteristic of hypnosis or hyperempiria should be far less daunting. (We can't all be Fred Astaire or Ginger Rogers, but most of us like to dance—and most of us, with practice, will sooner or later become pretty good at it!)

9 Concluding the Trance Experience

As in traditional hypnosis, the procedure for ending a hyperempiric experience involves providing suggestions which are timed and worded in such a way as to facilitate the mental transition back to the world of everyday awareness. Because repetition is so important for lasting learning, it is also helpful (at least for the first two or three times you guide the participant into hyperempiria) that you include some final suggestions which define how the experience will be perceived, interpreted, and remembered. The first few times (using your own words, of course), you might say something like this:

"Now I'm going to count backwards from ten to one, and by the count of one you will be all the way back to the usual, everyday state of consciousness in which we spend most of our waking lives. And whenever you want to, we can return again and again to this separate reality of trance, to create any experience you may desire.

"When you return, your mind will be clear and alert, and you will be feeling absolutely wonderful. You will remember clearly everything that has happened, and you will be thrilled and delighted by everything that you have experienced.

"Ten. You are beginning to return to the everyday state of consciousness now, as I begin the count back to one. Nine. Coming down more and more now, and feeling perfectly marvelous as you continue to return. Eight....Seven...Six...Soon you will be all the way back, feeling calm and refreshed, remembering clearly everything that happened while you were in hyperempiria. Five…Four…Almost back now. Three. Two. One. You can open your eyes now, feeling wonderful. You can open your eyes, feeling **wonderful!**"

After the first few times, the return can be shortened, somewhat as follows:

"And now, as I begin to count backwards from five to one, you are beginning to return from trance. Five. Coming back now. And by the time I get to the count of one, you will be all the way down. Four. Coming back more and more now. Soon you will be all the way back, glowing and radiant with joy. Three. Almost back now. Two. Almost ready to open your eyes. One. Now you can open your eyes, feeling wonderful. You can open your eyes now, feeling **wonderful!**"

When the "Enchanted Cottage" induction is used (and especially if the participant is a child) it is desirable to use the following suggestions to terminate the procedure:

"In just a moment, we are going to leave the enchanted cottage, and go back through the woods to the world outside. But you will remember everything that has happened here, and everything I have told you. And the things I have told you while we were here in the magic cottage will continue to be true, even when we return. But best of all, we will be able to come back to this special place whenever I tell you the magic story that takes us there.

"Now we are going out of the door of the enchanted cottage and starting back along the path. We are entering the woods now, and hurrying back along the way we came. Now we are beside the enchanted stream from which we drank. And soon we will be back in the world we left before I started to tell you the magic story, feeling thrilled and happy because of al the wonderful things that have happened to us.

"We're almost back now. Soon you will be able to open your eyes, feeling wonderful. Almost ready to open your eyes. Ready. Now we are back, and you can open your eyes, feeling **wonderful!**"

Possible After-Effects of Trance Experience

Even though you have specifically suggested that the participant is going to feel "wonderful" after the trance experience has been concluded, if the degree of involvement with the suggestion that their conscious processes were functioning differently has been strong enough, the **implications** of this latter suggestion can, on rare occasions, leave the participant with some degree of discomfort. These occasional aftereffects tend to be of brief duration and of mild to moderate intensity (Hilgard, 1974; Hilgard, Hilgard & Newman, 1961), although there is one account of the persistence of a posthypnotic dissociative reaction because of the opportunities afforded by this response for the expression of strong passive-aggressive tendencies within the subject's own personality (Starker, 1974). In other words, if a person has been inclined to assume that a trance experience is tiresome or stressful to some degree, responding successfully to an induction procedure will *cause* that person to experience feelings of stress or fatigue, just as if these feelings had been directly suggested. Usually, the effect of these implicit expectations can be countered by direct suggestions of well-being in the procedure for terminating the trance experience; but occasionally the earlier impressions are sufficiently strong that additional suggestions may be necessary to cancel their effects.

Often, when a participant merely reports a slight feeling of dizziness or fatigue, it is sufficient merely to remark, "That will go away in a minute or two—it won't last," and then to inquire after a few moments have elapsed whether or not the participant's distress is actually gone. If the participant still reports such feelings, you can ask the participant to close his or her eyes and a more elaborate set of suggestions may be employed **without** prefacing them with an induction. For example, if the participant should report that he or she has a headache which they did not have before the trance session, you can request them to close their eyes and say in a credible manner, "Now, as I count from one to five, your headache is going to go away, and by the time I get to the count of five it will be gone completely. One. Your headache is beginning to go away now. Two. It's leaving, going away more and more. Three. It's leaving, leaving. Four. Now it's almost gone. Five. Now your headache is gone completely, and you can open your eyes, feeling fine."

Having just been exposed to a trance induction format, most participants find it quite easy to return to a mental set in which suggestions such as the foregoing are readily and easily accepted. If, however, the participant should report that some aftereffects still persist, then it may be necessary, if they are willing, to briefly readminister an induction that will enhance the credibility of the contravening suggestions. This is easily done because, having just been in a frame of mind in which your spoken words have been taken so literally, it is easy to quickly return to it. You can simply say something like this, in a calm, matter-of-fact tone: "All right, just close your eyes, and I'm going to take you back into hypnosis [or hyperempiria] by counting from one to five, and by the time I get to the count of five, you'll be all the way back, just as far as you were before. Then, speaking slowly, you can begin, "One. Going back now—going all the way back. Two. Going all the way back into trance. And by the time I get to the count of five, you'll be all the way back, just as far as you were before. Three..." and so on, up to the count of five.

When you have reached the count of five, you can then give suggestions that the headache or other after-effect is going away, i.e., "And now you are relaxing and your headache is beginning to leave. It's going away….going away…. going away more and more now—and by the time you return from trance, your headache will be gone completely."

You can then conclude the trance experience using the following abbreviated procedure: "And now I'm going to count from five back to one, and by the time I get to the count of one, you'll be all the way down and feeling fine. Five. Beginning to come down now, and feeling much better as you continue to return, as your headache continues to leave. Four. Relaxed, and feeling fine. Three….Two….Almost back now, and ready to open your eyes. One. You can open your eyes now—feeling **wonderful!** (This last sentence can be repeated once more, for additional effect, even after the participant's eyes have opened.) Then, you can ask confidently, "You're feeling good now, aren't you?" And if the answer is anything less than an unqualified yes, the assurance can be repeated, "That should take care of itself in just a few moments now."

If the after-effects should still persist, you may want to wait a bit longer for them to "wear off," and be ready to repeat the process of a full return to trance. However, such an offer is likely to be declined, because if any distress should ever last this long, it is probably because there is some aspect of the trance experience itself, or possibly some aspect of your relationship, which may not even be consciously realized, and which will need to be explored and removed before you will be able to proceed.

Rapid Return to Trance

As time goes on, you will probably find that a participant who responds well to suggestion can be guided into trance more and more rapidly, without going through all of the imagery and suggestions that one normally uses with beginners, although some do still prefer to take their time and go the full route, primarily because the induction procedure itself is inherently pleasant. Generally, however, once a participant has become sufficiently accustomed to trance experience, all you need to do is to suggest during trance that at a mutually agreed-upon signal, the trance will be re-instated. You might say, for example: "Whenever you are ready for me to guide you back into trance in the future, all I will have to do is to place both my hands on your shoulders and look you in the eyes, and say, 'go back into trance,' and you will instantly return to trance, just as deep [or high] as you are right now."

Sometimes you might have to help this suggestion along a bit, especially at first, by adding additional suggestions: "Your eyes are ready to close now, and you can go back into trance, just as you were before....That's right....Your eyes are closing now, and soon they will be all the way closed." By the same token, after the participant's eyes have closed, you may want to incorporate a few phrases from the deepening or heightening procedures, to be sure that a sufficient degree of involvement with the trance procedure has been attained before proceeding further.

10 The Best Me Technique for Scripting Experience

The Best Me technique is derived from the principles of cognitive psychology (Beck, Rush, Shaw, & Emery, 1979; Lazarus, 1989). Use of this technique helps to insure that every major component of experience, i.e., orienting beliefs, emotions, sensations, automatic thoughts, memories, and expectations for the future, all contribute to the participant's greatest possible involvement with the situations you suggest. Taken together, these components form the acronym, "Best Me," which enables one to keep the major points easily in mind while guiding the participant's experiences in trance. Best Me suggestions may be presented in any order, and not every element of experience may be represented in every situation.

Orienting Beliefs, which set the stage for experience, include beliefs which orient one to person, place, and time. These include beliefs about who and where you are, about what is going on around you, and what has happened in the past which contributed to who and where you are.

Expectations may be modified by means of suggestion to operate as a form of self fulfilling prophecy which defines what is about to happen next, and the manner in which these events will be experienced and interpreted later in memory.

Sensations and perceptions, in various combinations, can be suggested with an intensity often approximating, and possibly even exceeding, those of real events.

Automatic *Thoughts* and images, in contrast to basic beliefs, operate almost constantly to keep us oriented to what is going on; but they usually occur so rapidly that they are hardly noticed. These, along with our more deliberate, conscious thought processes, may be enlisted to provide autosuggestions which support and enhance the suggestions which you provide, in much the same way that a chorus enhances a song.

Motives may either be suggested directly or as an implied consequence of other suggestions.

Emotions which occur naturally in response to suggested events may also be enriched by means of suggestion, and new emotions may be added and blended as well.

The remaining chapters in this book are devoted to a discussion of specific applications of the Best Me technique, and of an alternative paradigm which is necessary if the fullest potential of this technique is to be realized.

11 Breaking the Tyranny of the Future

Part of the problem in what is commonly referred to as "will power" lies in the discrepancy between the desirability of a long-term goal (losing weight, stopping smoking, or improving one's desire to study, for example), and the short-term frustration which is experienced in striving to attain it. Just as daydreaming about something we long for can inspire us to work harder by sharpening up our perceptions of the goal and how much we want it, and by giving us a taste of how we are going to feel when the goal is finally ours, the Best Me technique can do much the same thing (only much more clearly and much more intensely), by allowing us to experience now, in the present, many of the satisfactions which are normally associated only with goal attainment. While existing procedures (fantasy trips, guided imagery, and the like) may make use of many or even all of these components in varying degrees, use of the Best Me technique within a trance setting can facilitate goal-directed behavior through a more comprehensive experiential involvement in its imagined consequences.

Illustrative Case

"Alice" was a substance abuse counselor with a history of alcohol and drug dependency who sought help in order to stop smoking. "It's my twenty-fifth birthday tomorrow," she told me, "and I think this is a perfect time to quit." She had been free of her alcohol and drug habits for six years; but she had been smoking tobacco for "as long as she could remember," and had quit only once before, at the age of sixteen. She had resumed smoking three months later when she suddenly borrowed a cigarette from one of her friends, who was smoking at the time. She had made no more serious attempts to quit; and she presently smoked about a pack a day. Her steady boyfriend was an ex-smoker who was "into fitness," and was supportive of her desire to stop; but Alice was firm in her conviction that her desire to quit smoking was her own.

Since she was a substance abuse counselor, Alice was already familiar with such cognitive-behavioral concepts as automatic thoughts, trigger stimuli, and the importance of controlling the environment in order to maximize the probabilities of success. Using limited self-disclosure (J. Beck, 1995, p. 165), I told her that I had been a smoker for thirty years, and had tried to quit numerous times before I finally was able to do so. I attributed my own abstinence from tobacco for the past ten years to the fact that I had learned to modify my automatic thoughts about smoking, and the underlying beliefs which produced them. I asked her if she would be willing to use a cognitive-behavioral approach to work on her smoking habit, with the addition of hypnosis to make the technique even faster and more effective. Alice replied that she would. I reminded her that from her own work, she knew that the course of progress was almost never entirely smooth, and she should not be surprised if setbacks should occur, as there is obviously no such thing as a "miracle cure." Nevertheless, I assured her, I was confident that as long as she was willing to continue to work on the problem, making and testing hypotheses concerning the best way to eliminate her smoking habit, I had no doubt that we would ultimately succeed.

In response to further questions, Alice indicated that she had never been hypnotized before, and that she had no particular questions about it. Then, after describing the process of hypnosis, I asked Alice if she would have any trouble picturing herself relaxing on a soft, pink cloud for hypnotic imagery. She replied that she would not, and I proceeded with a traditional hypnotic induction, using the aforementioned imagery and slowly counting from one to ten, with suggestions of progressively increasing relaxation, drowsiness, comfort, and well-being, concluding with suggestions that she was now in a state of hypnosis.

Alice appeared to respond to the hypnotic procedure very well. Since she had been conditioned not to expect immediate success, we were able to assess her reaction to various types of suggestions without too much pressure for an immediate cessation of smoking. I suggested that as a result of her hypnotic experience this afternoon, her desire to smoke would be considerably diminished, to the point where it might even completely vanish; and that the situations which normally might make her want to smoke would no longer be effective in doing so. I added that in the coming days, she would think of more and more excellent reasons to be glad that she had stopped smoking. I also suggested that whenever the triggering situations came up which would normally cause her to smoke, she would think of these reasons to be glad that she had quit. Instead of experiencing any cravings to smoke, I suggested that she would feel strong feelings of pride, achievement, and accomplishment at the fact that she had become a non-smoker. I then terminated the hypnotic experience.

As a "homework" assignment, I asked Alice to keep track of her experiences, thoughts, and feelings, both about having stopped smoking, and about her hypnotic experience itself. Then, after reminding her to remove as many temptations to smoke as possible from her environment, I scheduled her for a second session early the following week.

The following morning, Alice called and asked to be seen for her second appointment, as she was leaving for a one-week vacation in Florida the day after. When she arrived, she told me, "After our session, and on the way home from work, I didn't have any desire to smoke at all. But I had all this nervous energy! Going home, I was stopped at a stop light and this guy drove up behind me in a big van, with his bright headlights on. I wanted to get out and beat him up. Then, that evening, I was walking with a girl friend who was smoking, and all of a sudden I said, 'Give me one of those things,' and I smoked it."

I reminded Alice of the importance of trigger stimuli, and asked her about her automatic thoughts when she had borrowed the cigarette. "I'll blow up," she replied, holding both arms out along her body and curving them to denote a considerable gain in weight. But her use of the term, "blow up" also seemed to imply that not smoking might make her lose her temper, particularly in view of her feelings about the motorist in the van the night before. Alice agreed that she was concerned both about the possibility of gaining weight and the possibility that not smoking might cause her to lose control of her temper.

I told her that research had shown that the actual amount of weight gain among ex-smokers was not excessive; and added that the strength of her cravings to smoke would considerably diminish with time; and at the end of a month, she would find that they would only return occasionally (Lynn, et al., 1994, pp. 560-562). She looked relieved.

Alice's responses to my previous suggestions had obviously been selective. Although she had said that her desire to smoke had disappeared (if only briefly), any feelings of happiness over having stopped smoking and any new reasons to be glad that she had stopped were noticeably lacking from her account. I said to her,

"You mentioned that you had all this 'nervous energy.' Would you describe yourself as a high-energy person?"

"**Very** high energy," she emphatically replied.

"Do you think that the nervous energy and irritation might be out of frustration that the pleasure of smoking has been taken away from you? (Jennings, 1991). Alice agreed. "How about reframing that nervous energy as happiness, because you are so glad that you have quit?"

"Can you **do** that?" Alice asked.

"Without a doubt," I told her, noting how well she had responded to the suggestion that she would have no desire to smoke, and adding that she was bound to do even better now that she knew that she was not going to gain weight, and that her cravings were not going to last forever.

At the conclusion of a series of suggestions designed to induce hypnosis, I repeated the suggestions of the previous session that her desire to smoke would completely vanish, and that the triggers which normally would arouse her cravings would no longer be effective in doing so. I then suggested that from that time on, any nervous energy that she might feel as a result of not smoking would be experienced as strong feelings of happiness, fulfillment, and satisfaction at the realization that she had stopped; and that her mind would be filled with thoughts of how glad she was that this had taken place. I concluded the hypnotic session with the suggestion that I was going to count from one to five, and that as the count continued, she would find herself becoming happier and happier, until by the count of five when the hypnosis would be terminated, she would be as happy as she could imagine herself to be. This would not interfere with her ability to concentrate, or to carry out her daily activities, I added; but this was the happiness which she would feel because she was finally going to become a non-smoker.

At the conclusion of the count of five, Alice opened her eyes, and I asked her how she was feeling. "Deliriously happy!" was the response. Her subsequent conversation was filled with apparently spontaneous statements such as, "I really don't want to smoke any more," and "I'm really glad I came today." I scheduled another session two weeks later, when she had returned from vacation.

At the beginning of the third session, Alice told me that she had not smoked since I last saw her, but she did report experiencing cravings to do so. I replied that the difficulty with what most people refer to as "will power" lies in the fact that many long-term goals require a great deal of work over a long period of time, and the rewards to be gained from the achievement of the goal are usually not available until the goal itself has been attained. I then introduced the concept of the Best Me technique, and asked her if she would like to experience this procedure. She readily agreed.

Of course, the exact wording of the suggestions provided to a given participant in hypnosis will vary with his or her responsiveness to suggestion; but since Alice had shown herself to be quite responsive to previous suggestions, I was able to proceed in a fairly straightforward manner. At the conclusion of the initial hypnotic suggestions, I began the suggestions for the Best Me technique as follows.

Expectations. "Now, you are about to have a very rewarding and exciting experience, and one which you will remember fondly and with pleasure all your life."

Orienting Beliefs. "I'm going to count from one to five, and by the time I get to the count of five, you will be mentally transported five years into the future, sitting on the beach, on a warm summer day, and savoring all of the satisfaction of not having had a cigarette for all that period of time. You will always be able to hear and to respond to my voice, and I will return you to the present in a few minutes. But until I do so, if you accept each detail of the scene as I describe it, without trying to think critically, your imagination will be free to allow you to experience the scene just as if you were really there. So just let yourself relax even more deeply now, and listen to my voice as I begin the count from one to five.

"One. You can feel your awareness of the present beginning to lessen now, as you feel yourself being transported to a scene five years into the future, sitting on the beach on a beautiful summer day.

"Two. Your awareness of the present is continuing to become dimmer, as I continue the count, and you can begin to be aware of yourself sitting on that sandy beach, on a beautiful summer day, five years into the future.

"Three. As your awareness of the present continues to fade, you are becoming more and more aware of yourself on that sandy beach, late on a warm summer afternoon.

"Four. Almost there now, as you picture yourself ever more clearly, sitting on that sandy beach five years from now, on a warm summer afternoon.

"Five. Now, it is five years into the future, and you are sitting on the beach, on a beautiful summer afternoon, and you have not smoked in five years. Just picture the scene, and imagine yourself resting there."

Sensations and perceptions. "Let yourself feel the warm sun on your body, and listen to the sound of the waves in the distance. Your whole body is glowing with radiant health, because it has been five years since your last cigarette."

Emotions. "And as you sit there, reflecting on this accomplishment, your whole being is flooded with strong and wonderful feelings of pride, achievement, and accomplishment. It's such a warm feeling of happiness and achievement, filling and flooding your entire being with delight, as its intensity continues to grow."

Automatic Thoughts. And all the time, you are thinking how glad you are that you have been able to stop smoking so long ago.

"As you continue thinking how glad you are that you have stopped smoking, the feelings of happiness continue to grow, getting stronger and stronger, like a snowball rolling downhill. And soon, you will be feeling all the happiness you can possibly hold, and at that point you can signal me by raising the index finger of your left hand."

A few seconds later, after Alice's index finger had begun to rise, I continued, "All right, we'll hold it at that point, and I'll count backwards from five to one, and we'll bring those feelings back to the present.

"And because you *know* from your own personal experience, that you are able to feel just as good now as you will feel when you have achieved your goal not to smoke, any cravings for tobacco which you might otherwise have had will be completely smothered by the pride, the satisfaction, the happiness, and the thrill of accomplishment that you will bring back with you to the present time."

Automatic Thoughts. "Your mind will be full of reasons why you are glad that you have stopped smoking."

Motives. "And you will want nothing more strongly than to continue with this goal of remaining a non-smoker for the rest of your life."

Orienting Beliefs. I then counted backwards from five to one, with transitional suggestions interspersed to re-orient Alice to the time and place from which she had left.

"How real was that?" I asked, after I had terminated the hypnotic session and Alice had opened her eyes.

"Pretty real," she replied, appearing somewhat surprised at the question.

In response to a follow-up inquiry three weeks later, Alice indicated that she had not resumed smoking, and no longer experienced strong cravings to do so, adding, "I'm a non-smoker, remember?"

Alice subsequently left her employment where we had worked together, but returned about a year later. Shortly thereafter, she came to my office and told me, "It's my one-year anniversary, and I still haven't smoked. Thank you, thank you, thank you!" Although I did not converse with Alice in the months that followed, her smile and cheery wave as she passed my window appeared to communicate that her efforts to remain a non-smoker were meeting with continued success.

Discussion

Marlatt (1985) has found that the average period from cessation to relapse among smokers trying to quit is seventeen days. Although this was not possible in the present case, if schedules permit, it is probably desirable to schedule a fourth and fifth session, from one to two weeks apart, in order to cover the period when cravings for nicotine tend to be the strongest.

This application of the Best Me technique is somewhat reminiscent of Dickens' well-known story, "A Christmas Carol," in which the avaricious Scrooge is shown the folly of his ways with the aid of three spirits, the Ghosts of Christmas Past, Christmas Present, and Christmas Yet to Come, who transport him into the past, the present, and the future respectively, and essentially terrorize him into mending his ways. In keeping with contemporary psychological thinking, however, in this application of the Best Me technique, the Dickensian bogeymen have been replaced by a therapist whose function is more akin to that of a coach; and the necessary incentives have been shifted from a primary reliance upon fear motivation to a vicarious involvement with anticipated future sources of reward.

The process of daydreaming about a desirable future goal, which we all engage in from time to time, may make use of similar motivational principles. The difference between what might be termed "motivational daydreaming" and the Best Me technique would appear to be largely a matter of the comprehensiveness and experiential reality of the latter. But with proper coaching in the Best Me technique and sufficient instruction in the use of self-induced trances, it should also be possible to assume greater control of one's destiny by becoming a much more effective "daydream believer."

At first glance, the Best Me technique would appear to possess numerous potential applications in the area of behavioral regulation and self-control. Indeed, an ourside observer may well be inclined to ask, "Why can't you use this nearly total control over personal experience to simply 'fix' whatever problems your clients may need help with, and send them happily on their way?" The answer, of course, lies in the fact that participants bring with them to the trance setting not only their presenting problem, but also the totality of the personality traits, needs, and environmental circumstances which rendered the problem difficult to solve in the first place; and before we can successfully vanquish the tyranny of the future we must deal with the tyranny of the total situation. Alice's case was chosen for didactic reasons, because it allowed me to demonstrate the application of the Best Me technique to a particular situation, and not to imply that this procedure constitutes a "magic bullet" for the resolution of a host of personal problems. While the procedure does appear promising, the probability of success in a given instance is likely to increase with the comprehensiveness of the approach to the client's problem, as is the case with other procedures; and comparative assessments of the relative efficacy of

this technique in comparison with others will have to await the outcome of systematic experimental investigation.

Because the totality of control over direct personal experience
made possible by the Best Me technique is its primary distinguishing characteristic, it would appear that the potential of this
technique will be more evident in situations where the quality of
experience is of relatively greater importance, as is the case in sex
therapy, which is discussed in the following chapter.

12 The Best Me Technique in Sex Therapy

Couples who seek the assistance of a sex therapist generally do so because they are in need of help with a specific problem, and not because their relationship has lost its former luster. But these couples, as well as those who have sought professional assistance for difficulties outside of the sexual realm, are often eager to explore new dimensions of lovemaking as their difficulties lessen and they rededicate themselves to one another's fulfillment. Best Me technique allows sufficiently willing and responsive couples to combine the elements of sexuality into a series of ultimately fulfilling experiences which they will treasure among the warmest memories of their lives. And for those whose physical and emotional closeness appears to be almost incapable of further improvement, the greatest surprises of all may be in store; for it is precisely those who have the greatest abilities who also possess the greatest potential.

In preliminary discussion, the therapist might point out that when undertaken by responsive and willing lovers these easily learned techniques may be used to produce almost at will those heights of passion and depths of intimacy which many people may otherwise experience on only a few occasions during the course of a lifetime. By learning to harness the power of sexual suggestion to translate their every word into feeling, thought, and experience, the couple will be able to enhance the setting for lovemaking, evoke the proper mood, intensify both responsiveness and desire, increase the length, depth, and frequency of climax, and focus the feelings of closeness and intimacy to blend together all the elements of the act of love into a series of ultimately fulfilling experiences which they will treasure among the warmest memories of their existence. If the couple expresses interest in employing these skills in their relationship, the therapist can then discuss the information for participants concerning the nature of trance experience presented in Chapter III.

The following suggestions may then be employed as a means of demonstrating the power and versatility of sexual suggestion, assessing the couple's initial responsiveness, and stimulating their interest in additional applications.

Time Expansion in Sex Therapy

Because of today's compressed time schedules and the competing demands of home and workplace, couples often find it difficult to mentally shift from the hard-driven, no-nonsense attitudes of the office and board room to the relaxed, playful, and caring mind set which is necessary for total sexual fulfillment. Upon reflection, most of us are aware that the sense of the passage of time is actually a subjective phenomenon; for sometimes a day can seem to go by in just a few minutes, or an hour may appear to be almost endless. The following suggestions for time expansion help to convert the experience of lovemaking into a "mini-vacation" which can enhance the enjoyment of virtually all couples, whether harried or not, who are sufficiently open to each other and responsive to suggestion. (Note the frequent use of repetition and redundancy, in order to heighten the effectiveness of the suggestions.)

"From now on, the time you spend in making love will seem to be passing much more slowly, and every part of your lovemaking is going to be infinitely more satisfying and more fulfilling because it will seem to last so much longer. You will feel as if you have all the time you need to savor each other's every touch and caress. You will feel as if you have all the time you need to fill your thoughts, your feelings, and your emotions with all the joys of your togetherness. And without anything to hold them back, all the love, and joy, and passion, and desire that you have for each other will be yours to enjoy to the fullest. Because time is flowing by so slowly for you, every aspect of your lovemaking will just seem to go on, and on, and on, giving you more pleasure and more joy than you could possibly imagine. And when your lovemaking is over, your sense of the passing of time will be returned to normal."

Lovemaking as a Form of Trance

It is often said that lovers "hypnotize" each other by means of a glance, a touch, or a caress; for they often seem so deeply enthralled by one another's presence that they appear to be almost oblivious to anything else. While the mutual enchantment which exists between lovers is certainly not hypnosis, it is obvious that there exists a high degree of rapport between them, and that their conscious processes are functioning differently! Thus, it is often a relatively simple matter to re-define their lovemaking experience in such a manner that the lovers are able to respond to each other's spoken suggestions as dramatically as if a formal trance induction had been provided.

After an appropriate (preferably hyperempiric) induction procedure and intensifying suggestions, which may be carried out either singly or together, sufficiently committed and responsive couples in an ongoing physical relationship who have received appropriate instruction in administering suggestions to one another may be given suggestions somewhat as follows.

"From now until the next time you make love, your love and your desire for each other is going to grow and grow, like a snowball rolling downhill—until, by the time you are in each other's arms once more, your love and your longing for each other will make you so tuned in, so sensitive, and so aware of each other's every want and need, that every suggestion spoken by either one of you will immediately be felt by the other, just as clearly and just as strongly as if you were in trance.

"When you are together again, you can both experience everything that your lover suggests to you just as if it is actually happening, because that's how close you're going to be."

"When you are together again, your love and your desire for each other is going to be so strong that you will experience each other as the perfect, ideal mate, infinitely more attractive and infinitely more desirable than anyone else could ever be. For as long as your lovemaking continues, you will be transported to greater heights of pleasure than you ever dreamed possible. You would not believe how strongly you are going to want each other, and how beautiful the experience is going to be.

"As you grow more sensitive and more responsive to your lover's every word and touch, your capacity for experience will multiply itself over and over, releasing every wonderful, positive emotion from the depths of your innermost selves for your exquisitely tuned bodies to savor and experience to the fullest.

"Great waves of pleasure, ecstasy, and delight will come gushing forth from the innermost depths of your being like water from behind a bursting dam, as you are guided all the way to the peak of your potential by the sound of your lover's words and the feel of your lover's caresses.

"Each successive wave, as it comes crashing forth, will carry you ever higher, leaving you ever more sensitive and more responsive to the one which is to follow.

"And when you finally fuse together in total unity, the waves of joy will finally blend together into one vast tide which will carry you up to an ultimate peak of fulfillment, more beautiful and more fulfilling than anything you could have imagined before.

"When your lovemaking is over, you will return to your everyday lives, feeling happy and totally fulfilled. But whenever you make love in the future, you will be just as close, and the experience will be just as special, as every suggestion you give to one another is immediately changed into reality in your lover's thought, feeling, and experience."

At the conclusion of these suggestions, the trance session may be terminated in the usual manner.

After the couple has become sufficiently familiar with the procedure just described, they may be taught to utilize self-induced trances in order to continue to explore new dimensions of sexuality after their professional relationship with the therapist has ended.

Best Me Suggestions for Sexual Enhancement

In utilizing Best Me suggestions, it is important to remember that since most people are able to fully concentrate on only one theme at a time, you should not try to emphasize too many different **kinds** of experiences within a single session. Instead, each lovemaking experience should be organized around one central concept. With repeated sessions over time, each one emphasizing different experiential themes, the total effect of the combined results can be dramatic indeed, as each theme is carried over to enhance responsiveness to the ones which follow.

Following is one example of how Best Me suggestions may be focused upon the central theme of commitment and used by a couple in a deep, permanent relationship in who wish to consecrate themselves to one another anew. For ease of illustration, the suggestions in this example are presented in the order B-E-S-T-M-E, and all of the elements have been included; but in actual use, they can be presented, modified, and re-presented in whatever order is best adapted to the needs of the moment, keeping in mind that repetition of suggestions previously spoken only tends to enhance their effectiveness; and not every element of the Best Me technique need be fully incorporated into every shared experience.

The suggestions in the following illustration of the Best Me technique have been worded as strongly as possible in order to demonstrate both the power and the potential of this technique. In actual practice, each couple should jointly decide upon what Best Me suggestions to use, in order that these suggestions may be completely in harmony with the totality of their present relationship and their style of communicating with one another. If this is done, the suggestions shared during the act of love are more likely to be totally believed in, as opposed to merely being momentarily believed; and the implications of such suggestions are much more likely to continue to function as self-fulfilling prophecies long after the lovemaking is over.

Orienting Beliefs. "I am your one, true, infinite, unbounded, and everlasting love."

Expectations. "And we are about to discover new dimensions of tenderness, ecstasy, and desire, greater and more profound than anything we have ever dreamed of, hoped for, longed for, or imagined, which will live in our hearts forever."

Sensations. "Each touch, and every caress of my hand, is making your entire body is becoming so sensitive and so responsive that you feel as if you are are ready to explode with joy."

Automatic *Thoughts.* "And your mind is filled with delicious anticipation of the fulfillment which will soon be ours."

Motives. "With each passing moment, our desire for each other is growing and growing, becoming stronger and more intense than we could possibly imagine, as we yearn for this fulfillment with every fiber of our being."

Emotions. "And if we lived a thousand years, we would not be able to experience a fraction of the joy, the ecstasy, and the infinite, unbounded love which is ours to share together now, in these golden moments: infinite, beyond infinity, and eternal, beyond all measure of eternity."

The Honeymoon as a Way of Life

Throughout this book, I have emphasized the fact that how a person responds to a suggestion at any given moment is a function of the total situation as he or she perceives it. Thus, the procedures described in this volume should never be seen as ends in themselves. Therapists are well aware that if lovers have come to share hyperempiric experiences of rapture, ecstasy, wonder, and delight, only to return to a life of bills to pay, appointments to keep, and an endless list of things which simply have to be done, the effectiveness of their suggestions will eventually begin to wane, regardless of how dramatic the results might have been initially. If, on the other hand, the lovers return to an environment in which romance comes ahead of everything else, and the first priority is the quality time which they spend with one another, then the joys which they have shared together in hyperempiria will be repeated again and again, as the conjugal joys of the honeymoon become a permanent way of life.

Escaping the Tyranny of the Total Situation

If momentary control over direct personal experience is a distinguishing characteristic of the Best Me technique, then in order to explore the full potential of this procedure, it may be necessary to apply it within an alternative paradigm which emphasizes the primacy of experience itself, as is the case with entertainment and the arts. In exploring the relevance of an alternative paradigm, however, I hasten to point out that we are in no way abandoning our values as therapists; for the ultimate purpose of art is fundamentally identical to the ultimate purpose of therapy: the facilitation of personal growth, the ennoblement of the human spirit, and the enrichment of human existence.

13 Experience as an Art Form

Many writers and investigators have envisioned a much greater degree of experiential involvement with various forms of artistic and entertainment media than exists today. Aldous Huxley (1958, p. 23), in his book, *Brave New World*, predicted that motion picture technology would develop to a point where it would involve not only the sense of vision, but all of the other senses as well, in a totally absorbing entertainment medium which he referred to as the "Feelies." Viewers of the Star Trek series on television, set some three hundred years in the future, are familiar with the concept of "Holodeck" programs: three-dimensional holographic images, with which the participants are able to interact as if the computer-generated images were actual people and events (Okuda, Okuda, & Mirek, 1994, p. 128). Currently, research and development of entertainment-based computer programs utilizing "virtual reality," or three-dimensional computer-generated imaging, is well underway; and several such programs are already in use (Burdea & Coiffet, 1994).

Anyone who has witnessed a demonstration of stage hypnosis will immediately recognize that all of the aforementioned phenomena can be experienced by sufficiently willing and able hypnotic subjects. In most cases, if the subject is responsive enough, such phenomena may be experienced merely by suggesting that they are to take place. But I am not advocating the use of stage hypnosis, which has as its purpose the entertainment of an audience. In a paper first presented at the American Psychological

Association (Gibbons, 1998) I proposed an entirely new paradigm for hypnosis and related phenomena, moving from a primary reliance upon a medical/counseling model to a concurrent view of suggestion as an art form and experience as an artistic medium. Just as a painter works with brush upon canvas and a sculptor works with chisel upon stone to create an esthetically desirable result, psychologists working with suggestion can also have as their purpose the production of esthetically desirable outcomes, working with the most exciting and versatile of all potential artistic media—experience itself!

While we certainly would not wish to abandon the current highly productive medical/counseling paradigm which has produced so many beneficial applications, consideration of an alternative model may also prove to be of considerable benefit to our fellow human beings, while simultaneously providing many additional professional and creative opportunities for those who may be inclined to pursue them.

Of course, since suggestibility is normally distributed in the general population (Hull, 1933; Hilgard, 1965), the number of people who may be able to benefit from the use of this alternative paradigm is comparatively limited, although significant progress is being made in teaching people who were previously low-responders to suggestion to perform as if they were high in the trait of suggestibility (Gorassini & Spanos, 1998). But, as is the case with other applications of suggestion, this should not deter us from making use of it. With an appropriately trained guide, individuals who are sufficiently responsive to suggestion may learn to respond to hypnotically directed experiences with a considerably greater degree of personal involvement than is usually obtained when one is reading a novel, or watching a motion picture or a play, and with much greater protection against the possibility of deleterious consequences than is available to people who are exposed to the excesses of contemporary media.

As is done with other forms of trance procedures, the purpose and basic theme of each directed experience should be thoroughly discussed with the participant beforehand, so that he or she has a clear understanding of what is about to take place. Such planning will help to insure the participant's wholehearted cooperation and will also assist in tailoring the experience to the participant's own personal tastes and preferences.

14 Implementing the New Paradigm

Though it is too brief to serve as a model of artistic content, the following vignette illustrates how Best Me suggestions may be employed with sufficiently responsive participants to construct a directed experience using either hypnosis or hyperempiria as a preparatory induction procedure. In actual use, of course, directors and participants will be able to explore some of the finest masterpieces of history, art, literature, and the mass media as active participants, tailoring these experiences to suit their own individual tastes and preferences, and perhaps even improving upon them.

After sufficient preliminary discussion and an appropriate preliminary induction, suggestions may be given using wording and delivery appropriate to the participant's ability to respond to suggestion. The following example may serve as a general guide.

Expectations. "Now, you are about experience an adventure which you will remember with enjoyment and pleasure for a long time to come."

Orienting Beliefs. "As your adventure is about to begin, one of the first things you notice is that time seems to be passing much more slowly than it normally does. Everything that is happening will be much more enjoyable because you will have all the time you need to savor every moment as completely as you like."

Additional orienting suggestions may then be provided (in the present illustration, to guide the participant in an experiential journey to a pyramid in ancient Egypt), worded somewhat as follows.

"Now we are preparing to journey backwards together in time, to visit an ancient Egyptian pyramid which has just been furnished with the most beautiful treasures of the Kingdom.

"In the centuries to come, the tomb will be broken into and looted several times before it eventually becomes lost beneath the drifting sands. But now, just after the current Pharaoh has been entombed and before the pyramid is sealed, you and I will be one of the few who will be able to view this treasure in all its splendor.

"You will always be able to hear and to respond to my voice, and I will return you to the present in a little while. But until I do, every aspect of the situation to which I guide you will be completely real, and you will experience it all just as if you were really there.

Emotions. "You can feel a growing sense of excitement and anticipation [*Expectations*] as you eagerly look forward to one of the most exciting adventures of your life.

Orienting Beliefs. "Your awareness of the present is dimming now, as we prepare to begin our journey. [Brief pause] Now, we are leaving the present and beginning to travel backwards together in time, backwards through the centuries, until we reach the destination which has been our goal.

"Now we are in ancient Egypt, late at night, standing directly before the entrance to a large pyramid which towers above us, its top completely lost to view in the darkness of a desert sandstorm. The darkness is so complete that the only light to be seen is a bright glow of torchlight coming from the entrance itself. The sudden ferocity of the storm has caused the superstitious guards to flee; and we quickly make our way inside in order to escape the ferocity of the storm ourselves.

Sensations and perceptions. "The passageway slopes steeply downward, and is lit by torches fastened to the wall at regular intervals. As we begin to make our way downward along its length, you can feel the smooth, hard stones beneath your feet as you listen to the sound of our echoing footsteps, and you can smell the burning wood from the brightly-burning torches as we pass them one by one.

Emotions. "And with each step we take, your excitement continues to grow. [*Motives*] You want very much to find the treasure which lies at the end of the passageway, [*Expectations*] and you can hardly wait until we reach the end of it.

Orienting Beliefs. "As we travel ever downward, plunging to greater and greater depths, [*automatic Thoughts*] your mind is constantly filled with thoughts of wonder and excitement [*Expectations*] at the marvels which we are about to discover.

Orienting Beliefs. "Now we have come to the very end of the passage, and we are about to enter the treasure chamber itself. [*Emotions*] And as we do so, you are thrilled by the beauty of the treasures which lie all around you. [*Sensations and perceptions*] Let's just stand here a moment so that you can take in the full magnificence of everything you see, [*Emotions*] and savor the beauty of all that lies before you."

After a moment or two, the participant can be prompted to describe the scene, with additional suggestions and narrative description provided by the director. Suggestions may also be couched in the form of questions which prompt the participant to supply additional content, such as, "Now, as you walk across the room, what else do you see?" or, after the participant has begun to describe a particular object, "We're walking up closer now, so that you can get a better look at it. Isn't it beautiful?"

When the treasure chamber has been sufficiently explored, the experience may be concluded as follows:

Orienting Beliefs. "Now, as we finish our exploration of this marvelous treasure room, we slowly begin to re-trace our steps up the passage and back to the entrance. And as we leave the pyramid, we find that the storm has abated, and the sun is just beginning to appear over the distant horizon. But fortunately for us, the guards are as yet nowhere to be seen. The sky is no longer overcast, and we can see for miles in every direction.

Sensations and perceptions. "Let's just stop and look around, to take in the full beauty of the scene before us....Feel the warm, early morning desert sun upon your face, and savor the freshness of the cool, dry air.

Orienting Beliefs. "Now It is time for us to return, to the place and timefrom which we left, [*Expectations*] for the guards will soon be back. But you will often find yourself fondly remembering the wonderful moments we have spent here, and eagerly looking forward to other adventures yet to come. And whenever you want to, we can return to this special place in your mind, and create together whatever type of experience you would like, which you will be able to enjoy just as much as if you were really there, and which you will treasure always among your fondest memories.

Orienting Beliefs. "Now I'm going to count backwards from ten to one, and by the time I get to the count of one you will be back in the usual, everyday state of mind in which we spend most of our waking lives. By the time I get to the count of one, you will be back in the location which we left to begin our journey, and your normal sense of the passage of time will be restored as well. Your mind will be clear and alert, and you will be feeling absolutely wonderful. You will remember clearly everything that has happened, and you will be thrilled and delighted by all that we have experienced together.

"Ten. You are beginning to return to an everyday frame of mind now, as I begin the count back to one. And by the time I get to the count of one, you will be completely back in the time and place from which we left to begin our journey, and your sense of the passage of time will be back to the pace of normal, everyday

life. Nine. Coming back more and more now, and feeling perfectly marvelous as you continue to return. Eight.... Seven....
Six.... Soon you will be all the way back to the place from which
we left, with time passing at its normal pace again, savoring with
pleasure and delight everything that has happened along our
journey. Five.... Four.... Almost back now. Three. Two. One. You
can open your eyes now, feeling wonderful. [with emphasis] You
can open your eyes, feeling **wonderful!**"

As previously discussed, Best Me suggestions may be used to
construct therapeutic experiences as well as artistic ones; and
many of the hypnotic techniques currently employed in clinical
practice (guided imagery, visualizations, fantasy trips, and the
like) can often be made more effective through the incorporation
of Best Me suggestions to enhance the experiential reality of the
procedure. A previous version of the trip to ancient Egypt just
described, for example, guides the participant in an exploration
of the treasures of one's own unconscious, with the suggestion
that he or she will be able to scoop up some of these treasures and
return with them to the world outside, so that they may then
"manifest themselves in new habits, new ideas, and new direc-
tions," concluding with the words, "And because your potential
for growth is truly infinite, each time we return to this treasury of
your unconscious, the storehouse will never be empty" (Gibbons,
1979, p. 158).

There is no shortage of material from which Best Me experiences can be constructed. Directors and participants will not
only be able to draw upon their own imagination and the professional literature for inspiration, but also the fields of art, literature, and the mass media, as well as the entire panoply of
recorded history, tailoring and adapting new experiences to suit
their own style, to co-create whatever masterpieces of experience may be appropriate to this new medium of artistic expres-

sion, recalling that the ultimate purpose of art is fundamentally identical to the ultimate purpose of therapy: the facilitation of personal growth, the ennoblement of the human spirit, and the enrichment of human existence.

References

Banyai, E. I., & Hilgard, E. R. (1976). A comparison of active-alert hypnotic induction with traditional relaxation induction. *Journal of Abnormal Psychology, 85,* 218-224.

Beck, A. T., Rush, A. J., Shaw, B. F., & Emery, G. (1979). *Cognitive therapy of depression.* New York: Guilford.

Beck, J. S. (1995). *Cognitive therapy: Basics and beyond.* New York: Guilford.

Burdea, G., & Coiffet, P. (1994). *Virtual reality technology.* New York: Wiley.

Cooper, L. (1956). Time distortion in hypnosis. In L. Le Cron (Ed.) Experimental hypnosis. New York: Macmillan (pp. 217-228).

Cooper, L., & Erickson, M. (1954). *Time distortion in hypnosis: An experimental and clinical investigation.* Baltimore: Williams & Wilkins.

Gibbons, D. (1973). *Beyond hypnosis: Explorations in hyperempiria.* New York: Power Publishers, Inc.

Gibbons, D. (1975, August). Hypnotic vs. hyperempiric induction: An experimental comparison. Paper presented at the meeting of the American Psychological Association, Chicago, IL.

Gibbons, D. (1976). Hypnotic vs. hyperempiric induction: An experimental comparison. *Perceptual and Motor Skills, 42,* 834.

Gibbons, D. (1979). *Applied hypnosis and hyperempiria.* New York: Plenum.

Gibbons, D. (1998, August). Suggestion as an art form: Alternative paradigm for hypnosis? Paper presented at the meeting of the American Psychological Association, San Francisco, CA.

Gibbons, D. (2000). *Applied hypnosis and hyperempiria.* San Jose, CA: Authors Choice Press.

Gorassini, D.R. & Spanos, N. P. (1999). The Carleton skill training program for modifying hypnotic suggestibility: Original version and variations. In Irving Kirsch, et al. (Eds.), *Clinical hypnosis and self-regulation: Cognitive-behavioral perspectives* (pp. 141-177). Washington, DC: American Psychological Association.

Hilgard, E. R. (1965). *Hypnotic susceptibility.* New York: Harcourt, Brace, & World.

Hilgard, E. R. (1974). Toward a neo-dissociation theory: Multiple cognitive controls in humanfunctioning. *Perspectives in biology and medicine,* 17, 301-316.

Hilgard, J. R., Hilgard, E. R., & Newman, M. (1961). Sequalae to hypnotic induction with special reference to earlier chemical anesthesia. *Journal of Nervous and Mental Disease, 133,* 461-478.

Hull, C. L. (1933). *Hypnosis and suggestibility: An experimental approach.* New York: Appleton-Century.

Huxley, A. (1958). *Brave new world.* New York: Bantam.

Jennings, P. S. (1991). To surrender drugs: A grief process in its own right. *Journal of Substance Abuse Treatment, 8,* 221-226.

Lazarus, A. A. (1989). *The practice of multimodal therapy.* Baltimore: Johns Hopkins University Press.

Lynn, S. J., Neufeld, V., Rhue, J.W., & Matorin, A. A. (1994). Hypnosis and smoking cessation: A cognitive behavioral treatment. In S. J. Lynn, J.W. Rhue, & I. Kirsch (Eds.), *Handbook of Clinical Hypnosis* (pp. 555-585). Washington, DC: American Psychological Association.

Marlatt, G.A. (1985). Situational determinants of relapse and skill-training interventions. In G. A. Marlatt & J. R. Gordon (Eds.), *Relapse prevention: Maintenance strategies in the treatment of addictive behaviors* (pp. 71-127). New York: Guilford.

Okuda, M., Okuda, D., & Mirek, D. (1994). *The Star Trek encyclopedia: A reference guide to the future.* New York: Pocket Books.

Starker, S. (1974). Persistence of a hypnotic dissociative reaction. *International journal of clinical and experimental hypnosis,22,* 131-137.

CPSIA information can be obtained at www.ICGtesting.com
Printed in the USA
LVOW06s1605280713

345022LV00001B/235/A

9 780595 173082